Francis Andrew March

Method of Philological Study of the English Language

Francis Andrew March

Method of Philological Study of the English Language

ISBN/EAN: 9783741186226

Manufactured in Europe, USA, Canada, Australia, Japa

Cover: Foto ©Andreas Hilbeck / pixelio.de

Manufactured and distributed by brebook publishing software (www.brebook.com)

Francis Andrew March

Method of Philological Study of the English Language

PHILOLOGICAL STUDY

OF THE

ENGLISH LANGUAGE.

BY

FRANCIS A. MARCH,

PROFESSOR OF THE ENGLISH LANGUAGE, AND LECTURER ON COMPARATIVE PHILOLOGY IN LAFAYETTE COLLEGE, EASTON, PA.

NEW YORK:

HARPER & BROTHERS, PUBLISHERS,

FRANKLIN SQUARE.

1865.

Francis A. March.

PREFACE.

CLASSICAL PHILOLOGY regards language mainly as literature, and studies grammar in connection with etymology, rhetoric, poetry, and criticism. A thorough method of philological study plainly has questions to ask of psychology, since the general laws of language are on one side also laws of mind; it includes the study of the history and character of a race and their language, and of the nature in which they have lived, since from these result the peculiar laws and idioms of a language, and the power of special words and phrases over the national heart; it includes the study of the life and times, and of the character of the author, since his idiotisms are a resultant of the influences of the age and his own genius; it implies the study of many books in many languages, since it is only by a comparison of works of different nations and ages that we can find out the peculiarities of each nation, age, and person, and trace the influences from which a great work has sprung, and the influences which it has exerted on other minds and on language. The science of language (Comparative Philology) has a still wider range; it seeks to know and reduce to system all the facts and laws of speech, and to ground them in laws of mind and of the organs of speech: there is no nook of man's mind, or heart, or will, no part of his nature or history, into which the student of language may not be called to look. An attempt has been made in this book to select such topics as may be taught to students in our high schools in connection with the critical study of a few English authors, and to arrange questions upon them, so as to enable a teacher to begin philological study without embarrassment, and to go on with it with success. The method is progressive. Similar questions are iterated and reiterated; the teacher should reiterate without end, that the dullest may be made to run in the right ruts.

In studying the life and times of each author, the students should look up information every where: scraps from novels like Scott's, from reviews and magazines, are not to be despised. The habit of investigating and writing out results makes the full man and the exact man at once; it divests composition of ninety-nine parts of its horrors, and it quickens thought ninety-nine times as much as beating the brain for original brilliancies. If, however, books are not to be had, the teacher should give the needed facts and thoughts in a lecture, and the students should take notes and rewrite.

There are many questions, especially among the introductory and the synoptical, which may be answered yes or no with little improvement; essays should be written embodying all these in connected discourse.

A large part of the questions call for comparison of the language of different authors, and of all with the English Bible. It is taken for granted that these greatest of English classics will be always at hand and in use. A special discussion of the language of the English translations of the Bible was to have completed this book, but has been cut off by want of room.

The figures often do not refer to any full answer to the questions; when reasons are asked for, or connection of thought, the student must hope to find little more than explanation of terms, and a starting-point for his own thinking. Fowler's English Language has more philological matter than his school grammar, and may be used throughout by means of Appendix D. In the study of Chaucer, and once in a while elsewhere, there are references to the fountains.

It is a good thing for those who are studying other languages to translate the English text into one or more of them. They should also be plied with questions on Comparative Grammar and Philology.

Many college professors wish to teach English, but can not get time for it. The Professor of Rhetoric, into whose hands this study oftenest falls, usually controls the writing of the classes, or some of them. Would not a weekly written exercise embodying answers to the questions in this book or to others like them, continued for a term or two, and followed by an examination, do something toward a thorough study of the English language and of English literature?

The name and form of this book are taken from the Method of Classical Study, by Dr. Taylor, of Andover, to whom we all owe so much.

EASTON, *Pa.*, *December*, 1864.

TABLE OF CONTENTS.

THE method is progressive. Questions on each topic, once begun, are kept up to the end.

ABBREVIATIONS.

√ prefixed marks a root; — prefixed marks a suffix; - suffixed marks a prefix; + suffixed to the number of a page or section means *and the following*, elsewhere + means *together with*; $<$ or $>$ is placed between two words when one is derived from the other, the angle pointing to the derived word; $<$ may be read *from*, $>$ *whence*; = means *equivalent to*; : means *akin to*; ⁔ over words indicates that they are to be treated in some respect as one.

Engl. means .... English.
Fr. means .... French.
Ger. means .... German.
Gr. means .... Greek.
It. means .... Italian.
Lat. means .... Latin.
M. Lat. means .... Latin of the Middle Ages.
O. E. means .... Old English.
O. Fr. means .... Old French.
Sanscr. means .... Sanscrit.
Semi-Saxon means .... Layamon.
Sp. means .... Spanish.

Figures alone refer to sections of Fowler's English Grammar, 12mo. In other cases they refer to volume and page.

Becker. A Grammar of the German Language. By K. F. Becker.

Bopp. A Comparative Grammar of the Sanscrit, etc. By Prof. F. Bopp.

Diez, R. G. Grammatik der Romanischen Sprachen. Von Friedrich Diez. 2[te] Ausgabe.

Dwight. Modern Philology. By B. W. Dwight.

Fiedler and Sachs. Wissenschaftliche Grammatik der Englischen Sprache.

Grimm, D. G. Dentsche Grammatik. Von Dr. Jacob Grimm.

Guest, E. R. A History of English Rhythms. By Edwin Guest, Esq., etc.

Latham, E. L. The English Language. By R. G. Latham, M.A., etc. 4th Ed.

Marsh, E. L. Lectures on the English Language. By George P. Marsh.

Marsh, E. L. L. The English Language and its Early Literature. By George P. Marsh.

Trench. On the Study of Words. By R. C. Trench, B.D., etc.

Trench. English Past and Present. By R. C. Trench, B.D., etc.

Unabr. Gram. The English Language in its Elements and Forms, with a History of its Origin and Development. By William C. Fowler, LL.D. (References to Sections.)

METHOD OF PHILOLOGICAL STUDY.

THE BEGINNING OF THE PILGRIM'S PROGRESS.

INTRODUCTORY.—Write an account of the life and works of Bunyan; especially of the Pilgrim's Progress, the circumstances under which it was written, its character, its influence and fame.—(See Chambers's Cyclopædia of English Literature, or Cleveland's Compendium of English Literature, and works there referred to.)

What famous Englishmen lived at the same time with Bunyan? Was he an associate of any of them? How old was he when the Paradise Lost was published? Does he show any knowledge of it? What important events occurred in England during his life? In America? Did he take part in any of them? When and where was the Pilgrim's Progress written? How old was Bunyan then? What scholastic preparation had he for writing a great work? What preparation from self-culture, preaching, writing? From religious experience? Had he, on the whole, been long and well trained for this work? What external circumstances helped him? His imprisonment? What books had he in prison? Was it a good thing that he had those only? Were the times favorable to such a work? How so? Did the Pilgrim's Progress take rank at once among the great works of genius? Does it now? On what grounds?

What is an allegory? 432. Had Bunyan scriptural example for this mode of teaching? What difference between an allegory and a parable? 432, 460. Are there any beings in classic mythology analogous to the characters of Bunyan? What difference between an allegory and a myth? Did Bunyan write other allegories? What famous English metrical allegory? What are the peculiar merits of the Pilgrim's Progress?

As I walked through the wilderness of this world, I lighted on a certain place where was a

---

(Study Becker's Syntax, 404–415, and Rhetorical Forms, 470–476. Write an analysis. A model is given in Appendix A.)

Read the first clause! "*As—world.*" Is it a leading or a dependent clause? Read the leading clause! "*I—place.*" What kind of sentence is it—declarative, interrogative, imperative, exclamatory, or optative? 404. What is the verb? 175, IV. The subject? 174. What words make the predicative combination? 405. *On* is the sign of a combination between what words? *Lighted+on place* is what kind of combination? 407. Does *on place* complete or extend the predicate? 408. Why so? Is it an adjunct of time, place, mode, or cause? 408. *Certain+place* is what kind of combination? 406. Is not *certain* superfluous? If so, have we tautology, pleonasm, or verbosity? 473. *A*+*place* is what kind of combination? 406. Colloquial form of *lighted?* What grammatical equivalent for *lighted on a place?* 412. Can you give a better expression? If so, explain why you think it better! What is the next clause? Why do you give "*As—world*" before "*Where—den?*" What kind of clause—subordinate or co-ordinate? 409. Substantive, adjective, or adverbial? 411. As an adverb it modifies what? What kind of adverb is it—of place, time, cause, condition, or manner? 411, III. What grammatical equivalents for *as I walked?* 412+. What is the connective? 396, IV. The verb? 175, IV. Subject? 174. Predicative combination? 405. *Through* is a sign of combination between what two words? *Walked+through wilderness* is what kind of combination? 407. Does *through wilderness* complete or extend the predicate? 408. Why so? Is it an adjunct of time, place, mode, or cause? 408. *The+wilderness* is what kind of combination? 406. Which note in 370 describes this use of *the?* *Of* is a sign of combination between what words? *Wilderness+of world* is what kind of combination? 406. Why so? Does *of* usually connect two nouns in an attributive relation? Is any other preposition like it in that respect? What reason for this in its meaning? *This+world* is what kind of combination? 406. Is *of this world* logically a partitive or appositive? 359, 362, VII. What grammatical equivalent for this clause, using a possessive case? 357, IV. Using an adjective for *wilderness?* for *of world?*

What is the next clause? "*Where—den.*" What kind of clause—

den, and laid me down in that place to sleep;

---

subordinate or co-ordinate? 409. Substantive, adjective, or adverbial? 411, II. What noun does it describe? What grammatical equivalent for *where* containing a relative pronoun? 412, 396, VIII. What is the connective? 396, IV. The verb? 175, IV. Subject? 174. Predicate? 353, 408. Of the three predications mentioned in 353 as possible, which is this? Can not position be predicated? Can an adverb of place be a true predicate?—(Unabridged Gram., 539, II., 5.) *A*+*den* is what kind of combination? 406. What peculiarity of collocation in this clause? 356. Is this case described in 356? A grammatical equivalent giving the present idiom for this clause? One reversing the collocation? One abridging this clause so as to include it in the former? Have the three first clauses the best possible collocation? Why not put the leading clause first? How could the others be arranged then? What objection to each arrangement? Can grammatical equivalents be used which will make the clause now first in place the leading clause? Would it not be better to say, *I was walking when I lighted?* Why not?

What is the next clause? What kind of clause—subordinate or co-ordinate? 409. Co-ordinate with what? (Name a clause always by giving its verb; *e. g.*, in answer to the last question, say, *The clause in which* lighted *is the verb.*) Is it copulative, adversative, disjunctive, or causal? 410. What is the connective? 410. The verb? 175, IV. Subject? 174. Direct object? 360. Predicative combination? 405. First objective combination? 407. What kind—completing or extending? 408. Is *laid me* a true reflective? 286. What grammatical equivalents for it? 374, V., VI. Would not *I assumed a recumbent position* be better? 473. Would not *I lay* be better? Why not? 473. What is the second objective combination? Is it completing or extending? 408. Why so? An adjunct of time, place, mode, or cause? 408. What is the third objective combination? What combination is *in* the sign of? *That*+*place* is what kind of combination? 406. What grammatical equivalent for *in that place?* 412. Would it not be better rhetorically not to repeat the word *place?* Why not? What is the fourth objective combination? What grammatical equivalent for *to sleep?* 413, 5. Why is *to sleep* called an abridged sentence? Is the grammatical equivalent which you give for it a subordinate or co-ordinate sentence? 409. Substantive, adjective, or adverbial? 411. In what government?

and, as I slept, I dreamed a dream. I dreamed, and, behold, I saw a man clothed with rags,

---

411, 1, 5. Does *to* here have its proper force as a preposition? What force? 388, II. Can you illustrate by using a noun and preposition in the clause? Which is better here, rhetorically, *to repose* or *to sleep?* Why? 473.

Who is the *I* in this sentence? Is *walked through the wilderness*, etc., allegorical? 432. What is the literal meaning? The metaphorical? Is the language drawn from the Bible? (Judges, xi., 16; Psalm xxiii., 4; and study Cruden's Concordance.) Is *lighted on a certain place* a biblical expression? (Gen., xxviii., 11.) Is the use of *den* allegorical? What are its two meanings? Is there a biblical association intended? (Hebrews, xi., 38.) Is *I laid me*, etc., biblical? (Psalms iii., 5; iv., 8: Gen., xxviii., 11.) Did Bunyan have Gen., xxviii., 10+ distinctly before him here? Can you state a simile in which the Pilgrim's Progress shall be compared to Jacob's ladder? 467.

What is the next clause? Is it subordinate or co-ordinate? 409. Co-ordinate with what clause? (Name the clause by its verb.) What is the connective? 410. The verb? 175, IV. The subject? 174. Predicative combination? 405. Objective combination? 407. What attributive combination? 406. What name is applied in 385, VIII., 360, to an objective relation like that of *dream?* Is *cognate objective* or *factitive object* the better name for *dream?* Why? Is *dreamed a dream* a biblical expression? Gen., xxxvii., 5-10. Is there not tautology, pleonasm, or verbosity in this clause? 473.

What is the next clause? Is it subordinate or co-ordinate? 409. Substantive, adjective, or adverbial? 411, III. Completing or extending? 411, III. An adjunct of place, time, cause, condition, or manner? 411, III. What is the verb? 175, IV. The subject? 174. The predicative combination? 405. Does *slept* denote momentary or continued action? Why not say *I was sleeping?* 255. Why not say *while sleeping?* Why not say *during the season of repose?* Why not put this clause after *dream?*

The next clause? What kind of sentence—declarative, interrogative, imperative, exclamatory, or optative? 404. What kind of combination? 405. Is this anadiplosis? 435.

The next clause? Of what clause is *behold* the verb? What is its subject? 380, VIII. What kind of sentence? 404. The clause has

standing in a certain place, with his face from his own house, a book in his hand, and a great burden upon his back.

---

the syntax of what part of speech? 305. What is the verb in the clause with *and?* Its subject? 174. Direct object? 360. *Clothed* combines with what? What kind of combination? 406. *Rags* combines with what? What kind of combination? 407. Which word is the sign of this combination? *Standing* combines with what? What kind of combination? 406. Is *in a certain place* necessary to the sense? Is there tautology, pleonasm, or verbosity in the clause? 473. What combination is *in* the sign of? What attributive combinations with *place?* 406. What combination is *with* the sign of? What grammatical equivalent for *with his face?* 412+. What combination is *from* the sign of? *Face+house?* 406. Does *from* usually denote an attributive combination? What ellipsis here? 354, 403. Does *from his own house* mean *from home?* Why prefer the former expression? What attributive combinations with *house?* 406. Is *his own house* etymologically an equivalent for *his house that he owned?* What does *book* combine with? What ellipsis with it—*with*, or *having*, or *who had*, or *being?* 354, 403. Why so? What ellipsis between *book* and *hand?* What combination is *in* the sign of? What does *and* connect—two sentences, or like parts of the same sentence? 401. Supply an ellipsis after *and* so that it may connect two sentences! What attributive combinations with *burden?* 406. *Burden* is parsed like what preceding word? *Upon* is the sign of what combination—*burden+back*, or *borne+back?* Is *upon his back* equivalent to an adjective or to an adverb? Are the traits mentioned in a natural order—(1) *clothed*, (2) *standing*, (3) *facing*, etc.? Why repeat *I dreamed* at the beginning of this sentence? 435. Is it a poetical form? (Compare Longfellow's Hiawatha.) What grammatical equivalent to incorporate it in the next clause? Would not *I saw in my dream* be better? Grammatical equivalent for *clothed with rags?* 412+. Why not say *ragged?* Prov., xxiii., 21. What is the metaphorical sense? Isaiah, lxiv., 6. What is the rhetorical effect of *in a certain place?* 473. Is not *place* repeated too often? Amend the language, or defend it! Metaphorical sense of *face from his own house?* Luke, xiv., 33. What book is in his hand? Metaphorical sense of *burden upon his back?* Psalm xxxviii., 4. What danger from frequent el-

I looked, and saw him open the book and read therein; and, as he read, he wept, and trembled;

---

lipsis? 470. Can you supply, or omit, or alter any words so as to add to the perspicuity or liveliness of the sentence? 470+.

What is the next clause? What kind of sentence—declarative, interrogative, imperative, exclamatory, or optative? 404. What kind of combination? 405.

What is the next clause? Is it subordinate or co-ordinate? 409. Co-ordinate with what clause? (Name it by its verb.) Is it copulative, adversative, disjunctive, or causal? 410. What is the connective? 410. The verb? 175, IV. The subject? 174. By what figure is the subject omitted? 354. What is the rhetorical effect of ellipsis? 403. What direct object? 360. What relation has *him* to *open?* Why is the subject of the infinitive put in the objective? Is it usually the same when expressed as the object of the preceding verb? 388, VI. Government of *open?* 388, III. Does it complete or extend the predicate? 408, I., *e*. What grammatical equivalent for *him open?* Which note in 370 describes the use of *the* here? Why not say *that book?* What does *and* connect? *Read* combines with what? What kind of combination? 408. *Read+therein* is what kind of combination? 408. Composition of *therein?* Which pronoun is *there* from? 236. What grammatical equivalent for *therein* containing the pronoun *that?* 396, VIII.

Next clause? What kind of clause? 409, 410. Co-ordinate with what clause? (Name it by its leading verb.) What is the connective? 410. Verb? 175, IV. Subject? 174. Combination? 405. What is *wept* from? Is it a weak or strong verb? 276. Why not *wepd?* 85–87.

Next clause? What kind of clause? Subordinate or co-ordinate? 409. Substantive, adjective, or adverbial? 411. As an adverb it modifies what? What kind of adverb? Of place, time, cause, condition, or manner? 411, III., 2. What grammatical equivalent for *as?* 412+. Is not *while* more precise? Is it not better? Does *read* denote continued action? Is not *while he was reading* better? Why not put this clause after *wept?* What effect on the perspicuity of *and trembled?* What effect on the anadiplosis? 435.

Next clause? What kind of clase? 409. Co-ordinate with what clause? Is the order natural—(1) *wept*, (2) *trembled*, (3) *cried?* What rhetorical figure? 444. Which word is the connective? 410. The verb? 175, IV. Subject? 174. By what figure is the subject omitted? 354.

and, not being able longer to contain, he brake

What rhetorical effect has the ellipsis? 403. What biblical reference here? Acts, xvi., 30+. Is it an allusion? 433.

Next clause? What kind of clause? 409. Co-ordinate with what clause? The connective? 410. The verb? 175, IV. The subject? 174. What attributive combinations with *he?* 406. *Not* combines with what? Kind of combination? 407. *Being* combines with what? Kind of combination? 406. *Able* combines with what? *Longer* combines with what? What combination is *to* the sign of? Does *to* have its usual meaning as a preposition here? Give a grammatical equivalent for *able to contain* which shall use some other preposition? Is *contain* used now as it is here? What grammatical equivalent for it in use now? 412+. What is the biblical idiotism? 1 Corinthians, vii., 9. Explain the meaning of *contain himself!* What does *himself* mean? What does *out* combine with? Kind of combination? 407. Kind of adjunct? 408. What connection of thought between the common meaning of *brake* and its meaning here? What is broken in this case? Connection of thought between the common meanings of *out* and its meaning here? Forth from what does it mean? What combination is *with* the sign of? *Brake+with cry* is what kind of combination? 407. *With cry* completes or extends the predicate? 408. Is it an adjunct of time, place, mode, or cause? 408. What attributive combinations with *cry?* 406. What does *saying* combine with? *Brake+saying* is what kind of combination? 408. Completing or extending? 408, 2, *d*. What other name for a participle used adverbially? (Gerund, Unabr. Gram., 539, VI., 2.) How many abridged sentences in this clause? What grammatical equivalents for *being*, *to contain*, and *saying*, will develop this clause into four clauses? 412+. What rhetorical grounds for preferring the present form? Is it favorable to perspicuity? 470–472. To liveliness? 473.

Next clause? What kind of sentence in form? 404. Direct or indirect interrogative? 404. In relation to the former clause is this clause subordinate or co-ordinate? Substantive, adjective, or adverb? 411. How is it parsed as a substantive? 411, 1, 3. What is its verb? 175, IV. Subject? 174. Direct object? 360. Predicative combination? 405. Objective combination? 407. Peculiarity of collocation of *what?* 361, 386. Of *I?* 356, 1; 384, 7. What grammatical equivalent for *shall do* containing an infinitive with *to?* 271, 3. Analyze *shall do;* parse *shall* alone! 271, III. Does it here have its primitive sense of *ought?*

out with a lamentable cry, saying, What shall I do?

256, 272. State its precise meaning! In what mode is *do* when parsed separate from *shall?* 389. Is this the objective or gerundial infinitive? 389, 263. Whence is this language drawn? Acts, ii., 37; xvi., 30.

Synoptical. How many verbs in the active voice are found in the extract now analyzed? How many in the passive voice? What is the rhetorical effect of the active as compared with the passive? Which makes the actor more prominent? Is the actor necessarily mentioned at all with the passive? Is the management of the verbs in this passage well suited to lively description? How many nouns in the extract? How many descriptive adjectives? Are they noticeably many or few? Would it not embellish the style to use more—*e. g.*, "*As I walked solitary and alone through the waste howling wilderness of this sin-polluted world,*" etc.? How many descriptive adverbs? Can you point out how more might have been used with good effect? How many personal pronouns in the extract? Are they noticeably many or few? What is the rhetorical effect of using many? 222, 226, 228. Unabridged Gram., 291+. Are they signs of personality and life? Would it not be better to put *we* for *I?* 226. What is egotism? Is it usually lively? Why? How many independent, co-ordinate, and substantive clauses in the extract? How many adjective and adverbial clauses? What is the rhetorical effect of the substantive clause—*e. g.*, "*Saying, What shall I do?*" compared with the adjective—*e. g.*, "*Inquiring as to the duties which he ought to perform?*" 473, 474. Why is the former more lively than the latter? What connection has this with the remark in 474 about conjunctions? How many points can you specify in which Bunyan's syntax is specially suited to allegorical writing?

How many words in this extract not of Anglo-Saxon origin? (*Certain, place, face, tremble, able, contain, lamentable, cry.*) Is this a large number for good English? (See Appendix B.) Do these words contribute their share to the expressiveness of the passage? Can you substitute better words from the Anglo-Saxon? Are any of them not biblical? Do 43, 61–64, understate the expressiveness of the Romanic portion of English? Is the monosyllabic character of English (95) inherited from the Anglo-Saxon? Should Bunyan be expected to use a very large proportion of Anglo-Saxon words—from his education? from his subject? from those for whom he wrote? from his favorite books? from any other considerations? 15–22, 42, 43, 59–65? Is Bunyan's diction (his words and phrases) drawn from the Bible? Is this a merit? Why? What intrinsic merits has the language of the English Bible? Is it made more perspicuous by early familiarity? What of its associations? How many particulars can you specify in which Bunyan's diction is specially adapted to an allegory like the Pilgrim's Progress? Does Bunyan use any poetical forms? What one is found in "I *w*alked through the *w*ilderness of this *w*orld?" 491. What in the repetition of *I dreamed?* (Compare Longfellow's Hiawatha.) Is a peculiar regular recurrence of accent to be found in the prose of the Pilgrim's Progress? Can you give striking examples of it? What kind of meter is the following extract? 522.

"So they went up to the Mountains, to behold the gardens and orchards,
The vineyards and fountains of water; where also they drank and washed themselves,
And did freely eat of the vineyards. Now there were on the tops of those Mountains,
Shepherds feeding their flocks; and they stood by the highway-side.
The Pilgrims therefore went to them, and leaning upon their staffs,
As is common with weary pilgrims, when they stand to talk with any by the way,
They ask-ed, Whose Delectable Mountains are these?
And whose be the sheep, that feed upon them?"

(The length of these lines is determined by the sense; both halves of the line usually cut a foot. The incorrect punctuation is copied as showing perception of the meter. As dactylic hexameters the first two verses would be:

So′ they went | up′ to the | Moun′tains ‡ t' be|hold′ the | gar′dens and | orch′ards, the
Vine′yards and | foun′tains of | wa′ter; ‡ where | al′so they | drank′ and | wash′ed them.)

Does the dactylic cadence run throughout the Pilgrim's Progress? Is it specially suited to this kind of writing? What likeness in Homer's, Goethe's, Longfellow's use of it? What likeness to the alliterative meters of the North? 491. What of the capacity of English for dactylic meter in view of the Pilgrim's Progress? Was Bunyan a maker of rhymes and verses? Did he write any dactylic verses? Or know any thing of the classic meters? Was he a true poet? If so, why did he not write better verses?

MILTON.

THE BEGINNING OF PARADISE LOST.

INTRODUCTORY.—Write an account of the life and works of Milton; especially of the Paradise Lost, Milton's preparation for it, the circumstances under which it was written, its character, influence, and fame.—(See Chambers's Cyclopædia of English Literature, or Cleveland's Compendium of English Literature, and works there referred to.)

Was Milton's father an author? Was his mother a remarkable woman? Had he remarkable brothers or sisters for companions in youth? What religious influences surrounded his childhood? Who prepared him for college? While preparing, did he study hard? Read much? What favorite books? Is it supposed that Du Bartas already turned his thoughts in the direction of Paradise Lost? Did he write? What? Did his style show "vital signs?" How did he spend his time in college? What friends there? Did he write any thing of note? What in English? In other languages? How long did he stay in college? When did he say that *he cared not how late he came into life, only that he came fit?* When did he visit Italy? What had he then written? What illustrious Italians were then living? What acquaintance did he have with any of them? Did he there become acquainted with works on the same subject as Paradise Lost? What? When did he return? Why so soon? What eminent Englishmen were his contemporaries? Was he a friend of Cromwell? What great events took place in England during his life? What part did he take in public affairs? What did he write on such affairs? When did he become blind? When is the Paradise Lost supposed to have been first conceived? Was it originally cast as an epic poem, or tragedy? What are the main points in Milton's description of his calling to greatness in the preface to the sec-

Of mans first disobedience and the fruit

(Write an analysis. Study Poetical Forms, 477–541, and Punctuation, 542–504, as well as the sections referred to before.)

True musical delight consists only in apt numbers, fit quantity of syllables, and the sense variously drawn out from one verse into another.—*Milton.*

In what meter is Paradise Lost written? 500. Why is it called iambic? What is an iambus? 483. Why is the meter called pentameter? 500. Why is it called blank verse? 493. What is a cæsura? 483. Scan the first verse! Is any foot not a pure iambus? 483. What syllables make the fourth foot? Has either an accent or emphasis in correct reading? 103. What is a foot of three unaccented syllables called? 483. Where is the cæsura? 483. (After *disobedience.*) Does it aid the tribrach? How? Is the second foot a pure iambus? Is *first* a simple unaccented syllable? What is meant by calling the second foot a *quasi-spondee?* 483.

ond book of his "Reason of Church Government?" When Milton says that he must use "industrious and select reading" as a means of preparation for his great work, what does he mean? Does he draw thoughts from all quarters for his work? Does he imitate the diction and syntax of other writers? What does he owe to Du Bartas? The Adamo of Andreini? Cædmon? Other less known writers? Has he taken as much from these as from the Bible or Homer? What does he owe to the Bible? Did he use the English Bible? Under what religious influences did he write? Did he believe himself inspired? What traces of his domestic experience are to be found in Paradise Lost? What of his public life? Are any of his characters taken from real life? What effect had his blindness on his work? When was the Paradise Lost published? How was it received? Has it affected English literature? The English language? Is it properly called an epic poem? What other epics are there? On what other subject had Milton thought of writing an epic? How is the maxim that there must be unity in variety in every work of art applied to an epic? Has the Paradise Lost unity of time? place? action? characters? sentiments? language? What variety is there in it in respect to time? place? action? characters? sentiments? language? Has each book a unity in variety of its own? Can each book be analyzed into parts having unity in variety? How far can such an analysis be carried? To each sentence? Each line? In which respect is it least perfect—unity or variety? Variety of time, place, character, action, meter? In which is it nearest perfection? Harmony? What are its greatest excellencies?

What is the first clause? (*Of man's first disobedience sing.*) What kind of sentence—declarative, interrogative, imperative, exclamatory,

Of that forbidden tree whose mortal taste
Brought death into the world and all our woe

Scan the second verse! Is any foot not a pure iambus? 483. Where is the cæsura? 483. Scan the third line! Is any foot not a pure iambus? 483. What is the first? 483. The second? Does Milton accent *into* on the last syllable in other places? 1, 91, 545; 2, 277, 773, 775, 910, 917; 6, 614, 703; 10, 17. Where is the cæsura? 483. Is this the most musical place for it?

---

or optative? 404. In what other forms can prayer be expressed? What rhetorical difference between the imperative and interrogative form of prayer? Between the imperative and declarative? What is the verb? 175, IV. Subject? 380, VIII. What is its omission called? 403. What is the predicative combination? 405. Of what combination is *of* the sign? What kind of combination is *sing+of disobedience?* 407. Does it complete or extend the predicate? 408. What does *man's* combine with? Kind of combination? 406. What does *first* combine with? Kind of combination? 406. Is this clause metaphorical? Who or what is the real singer? What is meant by singing? What common peculiarity in collocation? 356, 1. What poetical license in collocation? 386, 494. Should any capitals be used in this clause? What? Rule for each? 564. Any other marks? 553.

What is the next clause? The connective? 401. What kind of clause—subordinate or co-ordinate? 410. Copulative, adversative, disjunctive, or causal? 410. What ellipsis? 403. Verb? 175, IV. Subject? 380, VIII. Of what combination is the first *of* the sign? The second *of?* *Fruit+of tree* is what kind of combination? 406. What attributive combinations with *tree?* 406. Can this clause be parsed as an abridged clause incorporated with the first? Which way of parsing is preferable? Why? Should this clause be separated by a point from the former? What point? What rule? 543. Should any capitals be used? What? What rule? 564. What is the next clause? What kind of clause—subordinate or co-ordinate? Substantive, adjective, or adverbial? 411. What noun does it describe—*fruit* or *tree?* Can the taste of any thing but the fruit be meant? What answer to this argument? Why say *forbidden tree?* In Genesis, ii., 16+, is it *eat of fruit* or *eat of tree?* What argument from the force of *the* and *that?* Which attracts the relative most? (See line 8.) Does *the fruit of that tree whose taste*, etc., exactly equal *that fruit of the tree whose taste*, etc.? What argument from collocation? 376, 2. What rhetorical figure in *taste of*

With loss of eden till one greater man

Scan the fourth verse! Is any foot not a pure iambus? 483. Where is the cæsura? 483. Has the syllable following it any emphasis? 103. Is its metrical accent strong? (Compare the syllable after the cæsura in line first.) Is the third foot a pyrrhic? 483. How does *one greater* differ metrically from *a greater*? What is the fourth foot? 483.

tree? 469. Is the expression *forbidden fruit* in the Bible? *Forbidden tree? Mortal taste?* Is *taste* used in Genesis, ii., 16+? Does Milton affect unfamiliar words and syntax for poetic effect? What does *mortal* mean? Is not *mortal taste brought death* objectionable? 473. What is the connective in this clause? 376, 1. Verb? 175, IV. Subject? 174. Direct object? 360. What does *into* govern? What combination is it the sign of? What attributive combinations with *taste?* 406. With *world?* 406. What is the force of *the?* 370. Should this clause be separated from the preceding by a point? What point? What rule? 543, IX. Any capital? Rule? 564. Other marks? What is the next clause? Supply the ellipsis! What is the connective? 401. What kind of clause—subordinate or co-ordinate? 409. Co-ordinate with what clause? 410. Can it be parsed as an abridged proposition making a part of the former clause? What is the verb? 175, IV. Subject? 174. Direct object? 360. Attributive combinations with *woe?* 406. What combination is *with* the sign of? What kind of combination is *brought+with loss?* 407. Can you give any argument for the combination *fruit+with loss=fruit and loss?* What attributive combination with *loss?* 406. What grammatical equivalent for *of Eden?* 359. Should this clause be pointed from the preceding? By what point? What rule? 543. Should it be cut in two by any point? Where? By what point? Rule? 543. Any capitals? Rule for each? 564. *Eden* is in Italics in Milton's own editions; why? 564. Any other marks? Is Eden the name of Paradise, or the region in which it was situated? Does Milton so use it in other places? (See end of Paradise Lost). What rhetorical figure is *loss of Eden?* 469.

What is the next clause? Subordinate or co-ordinate? 409. Substantive, adjective, or adverb? 411. What objection to calling it an adjective describing *loss?* As an adverb, what can it modify? What ellipsis between *loss* and *till?* Is it an adverb of time, place, cause, condition, or manner? 411. Should it be separated from the former clause by a point? What point? Rule? 543. Should it be cut in two? What is the connective? 396, IV. Verb? 245. Subject? 352. Di-

Restore us and regain the blissful seat
Sing heavenly muse that on the secret top

Scan the fifth verse! Is any foot not a pure iambus? Where is the cæsura? Is there emphasis on the syllable after it? 103. Should it have a metrical accent in reading? (Compare verses 1, 4.) What is a foot of two unaccented syllables called? 483. Is there any regularity of movement in the successive cæsuras thus far? What is the effect of this movement of the cæsura toward the beginning of the verse? Is it true that the earlier cæsuras give more vivacity and the later more gravity? Is there a change of thought corresponding to the metrical change? Is this grave opening, gradually rising, well suited for an opening to the Paradise Lost?

Scan the sixth line! Is any foot not a pure iambus? 483. Is *sing* emphatic? 103. What is a foot of two accented syllables called? 483. Is the second foot an anapest? 483. (In Milton's own editions the printing is "Heav'nly.") Does the sense require more than one pause in the verse? Why does harmony require a second pause if a first is made after *sing*? Is the third foot a pure iambus? Is it more like a pyrrhic or a spondee? Is the meter related to that of the former verses as the sense to the sense? How so?

---

rect object? 360. Predicative combination? 405. Attributive combinations with *man*? 406. How does *one man* differ from *a man*? 216, 369, VI. *Greater* than whom? Mode and tense of *restore*? Should it not be *restores*? Are there any capitals? Rule? 564. Milton gives *Man* a capital; why? What is the next clause? What kind of clause? 409. Co-ordinate copulative with what clause? 410. (Name the clause by its verb.) Connective? 401. Verb? 245. Should it not be *regains*? Predicative combination? 405. Objective combination? 407. Attributive combinations with *seat*? 406. What does *seat* mean? Is it still used in the same sense? (Country-seat.) Why is *Eden* called *seat*? Should not the traditive object of *regain* be expressed? 360, II. What one is properly implied where none is expressed? Should this clause be separated from the foregoing by a point? What point? Rule? 543. Should it be cut in two? Should it be separated from the following word (*sing*)? What point? What rule? 543. Any capitals or other marks?

Next clause! Does *heavenly Muse* form a combination with any word in any clause heretofore examined? Should it be separated from the foregoing clause by any point? What point? What rule? 543, IV. How is *Muse* parsed? Is *heavenly Muse* like a separate clause in relation to the following clauses? What part of a true clause does it lack? What fitness in calling it a *quasi-clause*? As such, is it declarative, interrogative, imperative, exclamatory, or optative? 404. Should it be followed by an exclamation point or comma? 548, 543. Rule? What

of oreb or of sinai didst inspire that shepherd

Where should the seventh verse end? Scan it! Is any foot not a pure iambus? What is the second? The fourth? What pauses? Which is the principal cæsura? Do the syllables following the cæsuras receive emphasis? (See verses 1, 4, 5.) Where does the eighth line begin and end? Scan it! Where is the cæsura? Does the syllable (*who*) after it take the emphasis? Why is it that a cæsura and an unaccented syllable may so well take the place of an accented syllable? Which syllable in the first foot varies from a pure iambus? In the third? What fitness in the meters of the last two verses?

kind of combination is *heavenly Muse?* 406. Is it a biblical expression? From what source? Is any real being meant by it? Is a serious prayer to the third person of the Trinity intended? (Compare verses 17+.) What precisely is the wish expressed by *sing?* Why use the word *Muse?* Any capitals in this clause? Rules? 564. Any other marks? Is *heavenly* or *Heavenly* better? Is *Heav'nly* best of all? Why?

What is the next clause? What kind—subordinate or co-ordinate? 409. Substantive, adjective, or adverbial? 411. What noun does it describe? Should it be separated from *heavenly Muse?* By what point? What rule? Connective? 237. Verb? 245. Subject? 376. First objective combination? 407. Does it complete or extend the predicate? Second objective combination? 407. Is it an adjunct of time, place, mode, or cause? 408. What combination is *on* the sign of? What combination is *of* the sign of? What three attributive combinations with *top?* 406. Meaning of *secret* here? Is it a biblical descriptive? Is *Oreb* the word used in the English Bible? (Nor in the Hebrew, Septuagint, or Vulgate.) Why does Milton use it? Analyze *didst inspire!* Parse *didst* alone! Parse *inspire* alone! Is *inspire* an infinitive the direct object of *didst?* Give grammatical equivalents for the two words to illustrate their relation? What kind of combination is *that+shepherd?* What is the force of *that* in relation to *who?* 370, XI. Who is the Shepherd? Exodus, iii., 1. Why call him here *Shepherd* rather than, *e. g.*, *prophet* or *lawgiver?* Is he ever called *Shepherd* in the Bible? Is it a reference to inspiration given him while keeping sheep? Inspiration to write what grand poem? Any capitals in this clause? Rules for them? 564. What is the next clause? (*Or that on the secret top of Sinai didst inspire that shepherd.*) What kind of clause—subordinate or co-ordinate? 409. Copulative, adversative, disjunctive, or causal? 410. Disjunctive from what clause? Should it be separated from foregoing clause by a point? What point? What rule? 543.

who first taught the chosen seed in the beginning how the heavens and earth rose out of chaos or

---

Where does the ninth line begin and end? Where is the cæsura? 483. What is the first foot? A pyrrhic? 483. How many accented and emphatic syllables in the first hemistich? What expression has such a hemistich? What is the fifth foot? (The first and the second edition read "Heav'ns.") Does the expression of the two hemistichs vary with the sense? Where does the tenth verse begin, and where end? Cæsura where? 483. Is *rose* emphatic? Is *rose out* a spondee or a trochee? 483. What is the effect of having the invocation end in the middle of a verse and middle of a foot? Does the poet seem to be borne on by weight of thought past the formal stopping-place? Does it keep us ready to go on? Is the syllable after the cæsura emphatic? What special reason here for making it so?

Should there be a point between *Sinai* and *didst inspire?* What rule? 543. What is the verb? 245. Subject? 376. Objective combinations? 407. What combination is *of* the sign of? Does Milton mean to express a doubt whether the true name of some mountain on which Moses was inspired is Oreb or Sinai? What and where is Horeb? What and where is Sinai? Memorable for what events? Is any reference intended here to the giving of the law? Does *or* mean *and* used distributively—*i. e., of Horeb sometimes, other times of Sinai?* Is *or* a real or nominal disjunctive? 401, II. What capitals in this clause? Rule 564.

What is the next clause? What kind of clause? 409. Substantive, adjective, or adverb? 411. What noun does it describe? Should it be pointed from the foregoing? What rule? 543. What is the connective? 237. Verb? 245. Subject? 376. What kind of combination is *taught+seed?* Does it complete or extend the predicate? 408. What preposition can be supplied which will make good sense? Does the idiom ever require a *to* before the personal object after *teach?* When? What kind of object does *to* oftenest denote? 360, 2. Why not call *seed* the traditive object here? What other object has *taught?* What does *first* combine with? What attributives with *seed?* 406. What is meant by *chosen seed?* Can you find it in the English Bible? Any capitals? Rule? 564.

What is the next clause? What kind of clause—subordinate or coordinate? 409. Substantive, adjective, or adverb? 411. Is it the direct object of *taught?* 360, IV. Should it be pointed from the foregoing? Rule? Any other point? What is the connective? 396, IV. Verb? 245. Subject? 381. Give the two clauses which are abridged into this one? What kind of combination is *rose+out?* What is the

if sion hill delight thee more and siloas brook

Where does the eleventh verse begin? Where end? Scan it! Where is the cæsura? Is it a natural place for the cæsura in a pleasant line? What variations from the pure iambus? In the second foot? The fourth? Is the second hemistich improved by the anapæst? How so?

---

primary meaning of *of?* (from.) Is it here used in its primary sense? What combination is it the sign of? What objective combinations? 407. Of place? Of time? Of manner? Does the collocation of *in the beginning* affect the perspicuity? 470. Is the word *Chaos* in the Bible? Of what philosophy is it a term? What does it mean? What passage in the Bible is here referred to? The Muse is invoked as having inspired Moses to write what? Is the beginning of Genesis a poem? At what time in the life of Moses does Milton seem to think it to have been composed? Is this figure of the shepherd Moses composing amid the solitudes of the mountains fitted to stand at the opening of Paradise Lost? Is Milton's thought in this clause different from that of Moses? Is the statement better than that in the English Bible? Any capitals required? Rules? 564. Any other point?

What is the next clause? Connective? 401. What kind of clause? 409. Co-ordinate with what clause? (That in which *sing* is the verb.) Should it be separated from the foregoing clause? What point? What rule? 545. Does the principle of 545, 2, apply? What is the verb? 245. Subject? 355. Direct object? 360. Predicative combination? 405. Attributive combination with *aid?* 406. What combination is *thence+invoke?* What grammatical equivalent for *thence* containing the pronoun *that?* What combination is *to* the sign of? What attributive combinations with *song?* 406. Why *adventurous?* Is there any rhetorical figure here? What? Any capitals? Rules? 564. Other point?

What conditional clause modifies *invoke?* 411. What is meant by *protasis?* 411. What is the connective? 411. Should there be a point before *if?* If not, why not? If so, what point? What rule? 543. The verb? 245. Subject? 352. Attributive combination with subject? 406. First objective combination? 407. What kind of combination is *delight+more?* More than what? Where is *Sion hill?* Why mentioned as a haunt of the Muse? What poems of the Bible were there inspired? Is the word *Sion* in the English Bible? Is *Zion hill?* Why not use *Mount Zion?* (Compare verse 15.) Any capitals? Rules? 564. Any other point?

What is the next clause? What ellipsis? What kind of clause?

that flowed fast by the oracle
of god i thence invoke thy aid to
my adventurous song

Scan the twelfth verse! Where is the cæsura? What fitness in the first hemistich in connection with the second of the former line? Is the movement such as belongs to waters "that go softly?" How so? Does not the foot *fast by* injure the general effect? How so?

Scan the thirteenth verse! Where is the cæsura? Is the pause purely metrical—*i. e.*, not demanded by the sense? What is the last foot? (Milton's editions read "adventrous." It occurs five times in Paradise Lost, —*trous* always making only part of a foot, and having an apostrophe only once.)

409, 410. Co-ordinate with what clause? Does it belong with the protasis or apodosis? 411. What connective? 410. Verb? 245. Mode and tense of the verb? Subject? 352. Attributive combination with the subject? Where is *Siloa's brook?* Why mentioned as a haunt of the Muse? Is it mentioned by any of the greatest poets of the Bible? Isaiah, viii., 6. What is it called in the Bible? How is it accented in Milton? Correctly? What were the streams sacred to the Muses of Greece? What group of poets and poems is brought to mind by this invocation? Did Milton suppose the book of Job to have been written by Moses? Any capitals? Rules? 564. Other point? 553. Why use the possessive of *Siloa* and not of *Sion?*

What is the next clause? Is it subordinate or co-ordinate? 409. Substantive, adjective, or adverbial? 411. What noun does it describe? Should it be pointed from the preceding clause? If so, by what pause? What rule? 543, IX. If not, why? 543, IX. Connective? 237. Verb? 245. Predicative combination? 405, 376, XIX. What does *fast* combine with? What combination does *near* make in *flowed near to the oracle?* What kind of combination is *flowed+fast?* *Fast+by oracle?* What are the biblical expressions for *fast by?* Acts, xxvii., 13; 1 Kings, xxi., 1; 1 Chron., xix., 4. Connection of thought between the common meaning of *fast* and its meaning here? Has not *fast* unfit associations for "the waters of Siloah that go softly?" Of what combination is *of* a sign? 406. What grammatical equivalent for *oracle of God?* Where was the temple? Why use the past tense *flowed?* What fitness here in the word *oracle?* Is there a pause at the end of this clause? What pause? Rule? 543, 544. Any capitals? Rules? 564. Other points? (Milton prints flow'd) 553.

that with no middle flight intends to soar
above the aonian mount while it pursues
things unattempted yet in prose or rhime

Scan the fourteenth verse! Where is the cæsura? Is the first foot a trochee? Scan the fifteenth verse! Where is the cæsura? What is the second foot? The third? What fitness in these anapests to express the thought? (The anapestic, from its strong movement, was a favorite meter for marching songs.—*Greek Gram.*) What is the fourth foot? Why can a trochee be used at the beginning of a hemistich better than elsewhere? What reason in the thought for using one here?

Scan the sixteenth verse! Where is the cæsura? What is the first foot? Why is

---

What adjective clause describes *song?* Should it be pointed from the foregoing? What point? Rule? 543. Any other pauses? If so, what? Rule? What is the connective? 237. Verb? 245. Predicative combination? 405, 376, XIX. What kind of combination is *intends to soar?* 407. Does it complete or extend the predicate? 408. Does *to* have its usual force as a preposition? What grammatical equivalent without *to* for this clause? 412+. What is the subject of *soar?* Why is it not repeated? 388, 6. What grammatical equivalent will develop *to soar* into a full clause? 413. What combination is *above* the sign of? What attributive combinations with *mount?* What combination is *with* the sign of? What kind of an adjunct is *with flight*, time, place, mode, cause? 408. What attributive combinations with *flight?* 406. Under what figure is *song* here presented? 458, 467. To what winged thing is it compared—*e. g.*, a dove, swan, angel? What is the literal meaning of *middle flight?* The metaphorical? What mountain is meant? Why called Aonian? Is it a name in frequent use? What is the literal meaning of *soar above the Aonian mount?* The metaphorical? Why should it have such a metaphorical meaning? Translate the whole into literal statement! What poets did Milton have most in mind? Any capitals? Rules? 564. Other point? (First editions have "th'.") 553. What is the next clause? What kind of clause? 409. Subordinate or co-ordinate? 409. Substantive, adjective, or adverb? 411. Of time, place, cause, condition, or manner? 411, III. What word does it modify? Should it be separated from the foregoing clause by a point? What point? What rule? 543. Any other pause in the clause? What connective? 396, IV. Verb? 245. Subject? 174. Direct object? 360. Attributive combination with *things?* 406. What kind of combination is *unattempted+yet?* 407. What combination is *in* the sign of? What

and chiefly thou o spirit that dost prefer before

---

a spondee better there than an iambus? What is the effect of the uniform cæsuras in the latter part of the three last verses? Does it express a uniform serious effort? (See question on verse 5.)

Scan the seventeenth line! How many pauses are required? Which is the true cæsura? Do syntactical considerations settle it? Is *spirit* or *thou* the antecedent of *that*? What kind of foot is the third? The fourth? How was *spirit* pronounced by Milton? (In Shakespeare and poets of his time it is usually one syllable = *sprite*. Milton uses it sometimes for two half feet, sometimes for one, as poets now do.) If *spirit* is pronounced as two syllables, where must the cæsura be? Can emphasis be laid on *dost*? Which is best here, *sp'rit* or *spirit*?

---

kind of adjunct is *in prose*? 408. What does *or* connect? *Rhyme* is parsed like what word before it? What kind of combination is *unattempted+in rhyme*? What grammatical equivalent will expand *unattempted*, etc., into an adjective clause with a predicative combination expressed? What ellipsis after *or* will set forth the abridged clause equivalent to *or rhyme*? Will it give the sense to repeat *or while it pursues*, etc., after? Can you express a predicative combination after *or*, while *unattempted* is used before *or*? Should there be a pause before *or*? If so, what pause? What rule? If not, why not? Does this clause carry out the figure of the former? What is the literal meaning of *it*? Of *pursues*? What the metaphorical? Is not the figure dropped in *things unattempted*, etc.? Are the rules in 430 violated here? Had nothing before been written *of man's first disobedience*, etc.? (It had been a frequent subject. See Todd's Inquiry, where many such works in Italian, Spanish, etc., and one in Anglo-Saxon [Cædmon], are mentioned as probably known to Milton.) Why, then, does Milton say *unattempted*? What is meant by *rhime*? Is the Paradise Lost rhyme? Any capitals? 543. *Prose* and *Rhime* have capitals in the first editions; why? 543.

What is the next clause? What connective? 401. What kind of clause? 409. Co-ordinate with what clause? That in which *sing* or that in which *invoke* is the verb? Should it be pointed from the foregoing clause? What point? What rule? What is the verb? 245. Predicative combination? 405. Direct object? 360. What does *chiefly* combine with? Has it a special relation to *thou*? What? Should there be a point on either side of *chiefly*? Rule? 543. Any capitals? 564. How is *O* parsed? 305, 402. What kind of sentence is it most like — declarative, interrogative, imperative, exclamatory, or optative? 404. Should it be pointed from the foregoing word? By what pause?

ıll temples the upright heart and pure instruct me

Scan the eighteenth line! Where is the cæsura? What kind of foot is the third? The fourth? How does Milton pronounce *upright?* Verses 1, 221; 2, 72; 4, 837; 6, 82, 270, 627; 7, 632; 8, 260. In what cases does he uniformly use *upright'?*

Rule? 543. Should it have a capital? Rule? 564. How is *Spirit* parsed? 355, II., 402. Does it enter into any predicative combination? 405. What name has been given in these questions to such expressions? Should it be pointed from the preceding word? If so, what rule? Should it have a capital? Rule? 564. Is the *spirit* here invoked a different being from *heavenly muse* in verse sixth? Explain the two invocations! Is this a true prayer? Did Milton believe himself inspired? Exodus, xxxv., 31; James, i., 17.

What is the next clause? What kind of clause—subordinate or coordinate? 409. Substantive, adjective, or adverbial? 411. What noun does it describe? Should it be pointed from the foregoing? What point? Rule? 543. What connective? 237. Verb? 245. Analyze *dost prefer!* Parse *dost* alone! *Prefer* alone! Give grammatical equivalents in which a substantive is used for *prefer!* Subject? 376, XIX. Direct object? 360. Attributive combinations with *heart?* 406. What does *and* connect? 401. What grammatical equivalents will give *and* two predicative combinations to connect? 412. What combination is *before* the sign of? Does *before temples* complete or extend the predicate? 408. What attributive combination with *temples?* 406. Is the thought scriptural? 1 Cor., iii., 16, 17; vi., 19. Does Milton mean that the *upright heart* is a temple preferred among temples? Is his language correct? 364, XII. Does the fact that there are similar expressions found in Latin and Greek justify it? Is it analogous to

"God and his son except,
Created thing naught valued he."—Book ii., 678;

and to

"Adam the goodliest man of men since born
His sons, the fairest of her daughters Eve."—Book iv., 323?

How does the belief that Milton deliberately imitated Greek authors in these passages affect your estimate of his greatness? Is the language that of the English Bible? Should this clause be cut in two by a point? If so, what point? Rule? Should there be a point at the end of the clause? What? Rule? 543. Any capitals? Rules? 564. Any other points? (The first editions have "th'.") 553.

for thou knowest thou from the
first wast present and with mighty
wings outspread

Where does the nineteenth line begin? Scan it! What pauses? Which is the principal cæsura? 483. Is *for* accented? What kind of foot is *me for?* 483. Does the pause help it fill the place of an iambus? How so? Is the third foot a spondee? 483. (Milton prints "know'st.") What is the fourth foot? Amphibrach or trochee? 483. Where is a trochee allowable? Elsewhere than at the beginning of a hemistich? Why not? Is this line fit to be used in this meter? What adaptedness in it to the thought and feeling? To the meter of the verses before and after? Scan the twentieth line! Cæsura where? What is the second foot? Are all the other feet pure iambics? What fitness to the sense? What adjustment to the preceding verse? What rhythmic effect of the pause each side of *and?* Effect of *outspread?*

Next clause? (*For thou knowest.*) What kind of clause—subordinate or co-ordinate? 409. Copulative, adversative, disjunctive, or causal? 410. Should it be separated from the foregoing? What pause? What rule? 543. Connective? 301. Verb? 245. Predicative combination? 405. Any objective combination? 407. Any capitals? What rule? 564. Other point? 553.

Next clause? What kind—declarative, interrogative, imperative, exclamatory, or optative? 404. Should it be pointed from the foregoing? What point? Rule? 544. Verb? 245. What kind of combination is *thou+present?* 405. What is *wast* called? 353. *Present+from first* is what kind of combination? 407. How is *first* parsed? What kind of combination is *the first?* 406. Is this use of *the* described in 370? What peculiarity of collocation? Whence is the thought? Gen., i., 2. Is the language that of the English Bible? Any capitals? Rules? 564.

Next clause? What kind? (Co-ordinate copulative with the clause in which *wast* is the verb.) 409, 410. Should it be pointed from the foregoing clause? What point? Rule? 543. Connective? 410. Verb? 245. Subject? 352. What combination is *with* the sign of? Does *with wings* complete or extend the predicate? 408. Is it an adjunct of time, place, mode, or cause? 408. Attributive combinations with *wings?* 406. Should there be points to segregate *wings* and its attributes? What points? Rule? 543. Does *dovelike* refer to likeness of shape or manner of brooding? What does it combine with? Is the language warranted by the Bible? Luke, iii., 22. Parse *brooding!* What is a participle used adverbially called? (A gerund. Unabridged Gram., 539.) What does it combine with? Does it complete or extend the

dovelike satst
brooding on the vast abyss
and madest it pregnant what in
me is dark

Scan the twenty-first line! Cæsura where? Does it cut a pyrrhic? 483. What is the first foot? The second foot?

Scan the twenty-second verse! Cæsura where? 483. What is the second foot? (Milton has "mad'st.") Does the making the verse cæsura a foot cæsura tend to connect or dissever the second hemistich from the foregoing? Why?

predicate? 408, 2, *d.* Expand it into a clause having a predicative combination! *On* is a sign of what combination? Attributive combinations with *abyss?* 406. What is the language in the English Bible which Milton is here giving his poetic equivalents for? Genesis, i., 2. Which gives a more definite picture of creation? Is definiteness a characteristic of the sublime? Should creation be represented according to the laws of the sublime? Which is more sublime, the description of Milton or that in the English Bible? In what particulars? According to what principles? What peculiarities of collocation in this clause? 494. Does it give a different sense to put *outspread* after *wings?* Any capitals? Rules? 564. Other marks? 555, 553.

Next clause? What kind of clause? 409, 410. Co-ordinate copulative with what clause? Should it be separated from the foregoing by a point? What point? Rule? 543. Connective? 410. Verb? 245. Subject? 352. Predicative combination? 405. First objective combination? 407. What is the antecedent of *it?* Parse *pregnant!* 360, 3. What kind of combination is *madest+pregnant?* 408, 1, *g.* Does it complete or extend the predicate? 408, 1, *g.* Why is *pregnant* called a factitive object? 360, 3. Is the distinction made by Becker worth making between an adjective as predicate and as factitive object? Why so? Is the language of this clause figurative? Does it carry out the figure of the former clause? What is the *abyss* compared to? With what brood is it *pregnant?* What rhetorical form? 458. Does the language rise to the height of the argument? Any capitals? Rule? 564. Any other point? 553.

Next clause as printed? Next clause? Which is the leading clause? (*Illumine.*) What kind—declarative, interrogative, imperative, exclamatory, or optative? 404. Verb? 245. Subject? 380, VIII. What kind

illumine what is low, raise
and support

Scan the twenty-third verse! What pauses? Cæsura where? What trochee follows it? Point out how the twenty-second and twenty-third stand related metrically to the foregoing and following verses? Do they give variety? Do they prepare the ear for a flowing close of this opening passage?

---

of combination is *illumine+thou?* 405. What of the collocation? 356. Should there be a point before *illumine?* What point? What rule? 543. Any capitals? Rule? 564. What kind of clause is *what in me is dark?* 409, 410. Subordinate substantive in what case and government? 411, I., 3. Should there be any point before it? What? Rule? 544, 545, 546. Verb? 245. What logical name is given the verb here? 353. What does *dark* combine with? What kind of combination? 405. What combination is *in* the sign of? *What+in me* is what kind of combination? 406. Does *in* usually denote an attributive? Is there an ellipsis here? Give an equivalent for *what in me is dark*, using only literal language? P. L., iii., 45–51; Psalm lxix., 23; Romans, i., 21; Luke, xi., 34+; Eph., iv., 18. Is *illumine* used in the English Bible? Is the statement in 376, Rule XX., about *what* correct? Is the sentence in fine print that follows the rule correct? Any capitals? Rule? 564.

Next clause? (*What is low.*) Next clause? (*Raise.*) Next clause? (*And support.*) Which is the leading clause of these three? What kind—declarative, interrogative, imperative, exclamatory, or optative? 404. What combination does it contain? 405, 380, VIII. Any point before it? What? Rule? 543. Any capital? What clauses does *and* connect? What combination with *support?* 380, VIII. Should *and* have a point before it? If so, what point? Rule? 543. If not, why not? 543. What kind of clause is *what is low?* 409, 411. As a subordinate substantive, what is its government? 411, I., 3. What is its verb? 245. Subject? 352. What combination is *is* the sign of? What name is given *is* in such propositions? 353. What is the predicative combination? 408. What ellipsis in this clause? Has Milton probably any particular power in his thoughts which he wishes *raised and supported?* Isaiah, xxix., 4. What point before *what is low?* Rule? 543–548. (After *pregnant* the first and second editions have a colon, after *illumine* a comma, after *support* a semicolon; no intermediate pauses.) Any capitals? 564.

Next clause? What kind of clause—subordinate or co-ordinate? 409.

that to the highth of this great argument
i may assert eternal providence

Scan the twenty-fourth verse! Cæsura where? 483. What is the first foot? 483. Is the fourth a pure iambus? The fifth?

Scan the twenty-fifth verse! Cæsura where? Is it required by the sense, or purely metrical? Which has more stress, *I* or *may*? What is the first foot? The fifth? How many pairs of unaccented, unemphatic syllables in these two lines? Does Milton often end a line with a pyrrhic? Can you find two other such lines in succession? Do not these light feet make the lines weak and prosaic? Do the cæsuras help the matter? Explain!

Substantive, adjective, or adverb? 411, I., 5. Becker calls it adverbial; which is right? As a substantive, how is it governed? What ellipsis may be supplied? What part of speech is *that* originally? 236. *Support that I may assert*, etc.=*Support* for *that* purpose; viz., *my assertion*, etc. How is *that* parsed in the second equivalent? How is *assertion* parsed? *That*, considered as a demonstrative, belongs in the clause with which verb? *I may assert*, etc., is in what relation to the demonstrative *that*? 362. What do the grammars call *that* as it stands in the text? 237, III., 4; 401, I. When is *that* called a conjunction? 237, III. Should this clause be separated from the foregoing? By what point? Rule? 544. If parsed as a subordinate adverbial clause, what verbs does it modify? What kind of adverb—of place, time, reason, condition, or manner? 411, III., 3. What is the verb? 245. Subject? 174. Direct object? 360. Mode and tense of the verb? Analyze *may assert!* 272. Parse *may* alone! 273. Parse *assert* alone! 389. Give grammatical equivalents for *may assert* such as to show *assert* to be an infinitive! Is it the objective or gerundial infinitive? 389. *I*+*may assert* is what kind of combination? 405. Who is meant by *I*? Does *I* take an antecedent? 373, 222+. Does it represent a name, or a person directly? Is *pro-noun* a good name for it? How does the *I* of Milton compare with the *I* of Bunyan? (See questions on Bunyan, p. 14.) Which is farthest from egotism? What attributive combination with *Providence*? 406. Grammatical equivalent for *assert eternal Providence*? 412+. What combination is *to* the sign of? Does *highth* complete or extend the predicate? 408. What combination is *of* the sign of? *Highth*+*of argument* is what kind of combination? 406. *Great*+*argument* is what kind of combination? 406. *This*+*great argument* is what kind of combination? 406. What does *argument* mean here? Give grammatical equivalents to explain the meaning of verse twenty-

and justify the ways of god to men.

Scan the twenty-sixth verse! Is it all pure iambics? 483. Cæsura where? In the same place as in the two preceding verses? With two light syllables before it? Where no pause is required by the sense? What can you say in favor of the meter of the three last verses? How are they suited for a close to this opening passage?

Synoptical.—How many spondees or quasi-spondees are there in these verses? 483. Is there any place in the verse in which no spondee can be found? Which verses have one in the first place? The second? The third? Fourth? Fifth? How many pyrrhics and quasi-pyrrhics? In what places in the verse are they found? Elsewhere than with the cæsura or the end of the verse? How many tribrachs or quasi-tribrachs? Are they found elsewhere than with the cæsura? Are there any anapests? Where? How many trochees are there? Are they found elsewhere than at the beginning of a hemistich? Why not? In what places is the cæsura found? In which place oftenest? Are any two of the verses exactly alike in meter? Is any pair of verses exactly like any other pair? How is the fitness of the variation determined? Is there any unity in the variety? Are there other sources of melody besides variation of feet and of cæsuras? Is there happy arrangement of vowel sounds—as long, short, etc.? Point out any verses that derive special beauty from that source! Is there metrical arrangement of consonants? What marks of Anglo-Saxon verse in the two first lines? 491. (*First—fruit—forbidden.*) Is there other art used in the disposition of consonants? Point out verses specially good in this respect! Does Milton use repetition as a poetic form? Give examples! B. 3, 178+; 7, 184+; 10, 850+, etc. Would not rhyme improve the Paradise Lost? Did Milton condemn it on principle? (Yes. See "rea-

---

fourth! Translate the whole clause, using none of Milton's notional words! 176. What poetic license in collocation in this clause? 494. Is any thing else in it poetic? Any pauses within the clause? If so, where? What? Rules? Any capitals? Rules? 564. Other punctuation marks? (The first edition has "th' Eternal;" *th'* was afterward struck out as erratum.)

Next clause? Supply the whole ellipsis! Is it subordinate or co-ordinate? 409. Co-ordinate with what clause? Should it be separated from the preceding by a point? What point? What rule? 543. What is the connective? 410. Verb? 245. Mode and tense? Analyze *may justify!* Parse *may* alone! Parse *justify* alone! What is the predicative combination? 405. Direct object? 360. Force of *the*? 370. Of what combination is *of* the sign? What grammatical equivalent for *of God*? 357+. What combination is *to* the sign of? *Justify+to men*, or *ways+to men*? Why? Pope says, "*Vindicate the ways of God to man*," which is preferable? Any capitals? Rules? 564. (Go on with similar questions through the additional verses: they are reprinted exactly from the first edition.)

Say first, for Heav'n hides nothing from thy view

son why the poem rimes not" prefixed to P. L.) Did Milton inherit a musical genius? How and to what extent was it cultivated? What was his favorite instrument? Does the music of his verses resemble that of an organ? Had he studied the meter of the best poets? In what languages most? What were his habits of composition? Does the music of verses in the mind of a poet keep in advance of his selection and arrangement of words? Does the meter of his early poems resemble that of the Paradise Lost? Does that of Samson Agonistes? Does it become more complex in his later works? Is there a rhythmical movement in Milton's prose? Is it like the movement of his verse? Study the cadences of the following extract from "A Speech for the Liberty of unlicensed Printing." It is provisionally divided in hemistichs according to the natural cadences in reading:

"Methinks I see in my mind ‡ a noble and puissant nation
Rousing herself ‡ like a strong man after sleep,
And shaking her invincible locks; ‡ Methinks
I see her as an eagle ‡ muing her mighty youth,
And kindling her undazzled eyes ‡ at the full mid-day beam;
Purging and unscaling ‡ her long-abusèd sight
At the fountain itself ‡ of heavenly radiance;
While the whole noise ‡ of timorous and flocking birds,
With those also ‡ that love the twilight,
Flutter about; ‡ amazed at what she means,
And in their envious gabble ‡ would prognosticate
A year of sects and schisms."

Can you arrange this passage into the same measure as the Paradise Lost? Compare with Bunyan's prose. (See page 15.) Is the movement here iambic? Which has the greater variety? Is Milton's harmony to be appreciated by an uncultivated ear or mind? Or by any one without long acquaintance with it? Is there any great musician whose style seems to you to be like Milton's? Which is the higher work of genius—a grand passage from Beethoven or from Paradise Lost? Why? Write an essay on the versification of Milton covering the ground of the foregoing questions.

Synoptical.—How many commas have you made in this extract? How many semicolons? Colons? Does each semicolon indicate a different syntactical relation from any comma or colon? Have you made any periods? Does each indicate a different syntactical relation from any other point? The first edition of the Paradise Lost has in this passage 21 commas, 3 semicolons, 2 colons, 2 periods, 73 capitals, 7 words in italics, 1 apostrophe used to mark the possessive case (not in line 1), 8 to mark contraction. The following words are spelt as here printed: "Tast," "adventrous," "Rhime," "highth," "justifie," "wayes." The second edition, which was corrected by Milton, and divided into twelve books instead of ten, is exactly like the first in this passage, except "illumin" for "illumine," and "th'" erased from line 25. Milton spelt *meter* with *-er*, so did Shakespeare, and the Anglo-Saxons, from

Nor the deep Tract of Hell, say first what cause
Mov'd our Grand Parents in that happy State,
Favour'd of Heav'n so highly, to fall off
From their Creator, and transgress his Will
For one restraint, Lords of the World besides?
Who first seduc'd them to that fowl revolt?
Th' infernal Serpent; he it was, whose guile
Stird up with Envy and Revenge, deceiv'd
The Mother of Mankinde, what time his Pride
Had cast him out from Heav'n, with all his Host
Of Rebel Angels, by whose aid aspiring
To set himself in Glory above his Peers,
He trusted to have equal'd the most High,
If he oppos'd; and with ambitious aim
Against the Throne and Monarchy of God
Rais'd impious War in Heav'n and Battel proud
With vain attempt. Him the Almighty Power

---

whom we have it. Can you make out where all the points are, which words are in italics, have capitals, etc.?

Does this extract abound in poetical forms, or is it comparatively plain? Is that in good taste? How many independent and substantive clauses in it? How many adjective and adverbial? What peculiarities of style are suggested by comparing the ratio of these clauses in Milton with that in Bunyan? Is there any thing in the form of the leading verbs in this passage which adds to the liveliness? Is the imperative mode an especially forcible form in English? How many verbs in the extract? How many nouns? Descriptive adjectives? Descriptive adverbs? Personal pronouns? Relative pronouns and conjunctions? What is the ratio of each to the whole number of words? Which parts of speech have a greater ratio than in Bunyan? How is the style affected by each difference, as to perspicuity? 470–472. As to liveliness? 473, 474. Egotism? As to its fitness to express the sublime?

What words in the extract not of Anglo-Saxon origin? (Disobedience, fruit, mortal, taste, Eden, restore, regain, muse, secret, Oreb, Sinai, inspire, chaos, Sion, delight, Siloa, oracle, invoke, aid, adventur-

Hurld headlong flaming from th' Ethereal Skie
With hideous ruine and combustion down
To bottomless perdition, there to dwell
In Adamantine Chains and penal Fire,
Who durst defie th' Omnipotent to Arms.
Nine times the Space that measures Day and Night
To mortal men, he with his horrid crew
Lay vanquisht, rowling in the fiery Gulfe
Confounded though immortal: But his doom
Reserv'd him to more wrath; for now the thought
Both of lost happiness and lasting pain
Torments him; round he throws his baleful eyes
That witness'd huge affliction and dismay
Mixt with obdurate pride and stedfast hate:
At once as far as Angels kenn he views
The dismal Situation waste and wilde,

---

ous, intends, soar, Aonian, mount, pursues, unattempted, prose, chiefly, spirit, prefer, temples, pure, instruct, present, vast, abyss, pregnant, illumine, support, argument, assert, eternal, Providence, justify.) Is this a large number compared with average good English? (App. B.) Compared with the passage from Bunyan before examined? Compared with other parts of Paradise Lost? Compared with Milton's prose writings? What external circumstances would be likely to make Milton's language abound in words not Anglo-Saxon? What the effect of the place in which he lived—*e. g.*, city or country, England or elsewhere? What the effect of time—*e. g.*, the habit of the age to use much or little learned language? What the effect of the rank and manners of his family? Which rank use most Norman? What of his education, habits of study, profession? What of his associates and favorite authors? What of the class of persons for whom he wrote, "fit audience, though few?" What the effect of the subjects on which he wrote? Was he used to writing in other languages than English? What internal (subjective) reasons for his use of much foreign diction? Any qualities of the blood: was he Saxon, Norman, or Celt? What points in his character affect his language? Was he, *e. g.*, rather sensitive or reflective? Simple or grand? Humorous? Ambitious of literary superiority and originali-

A Dungeon horrible, on all sides round
As one great Furnace flam'd, yet from those flames
No light, but rather darkness visible
Serv'd only to discover sights of woe,
Regions of sorrow, doleful shades, where peace
And rest can never dwell, hope never comes
That comes to all; but torture without end
Still urges, and a fiery Deluge, fed
With ever-burning Sulphur unconsum'd:
Such place Eternal Justice had prepar'd
For those rebellious, here their portion set
As far remov'd from God and light of Heav'n
As from the Center thrice to th' utmost Pole.

---

ty? Musical? Rhetorical? Will you show how each of these traits worked on his language? Do the Romanic words add to the beauty of this passage? Can you substitute a better Anglo-Saxon word for any of them? Can you substitute a better Romanic word for any Anglo-Saxon word in the passage? Is Milton's language "a new language," as Johnson says? (Lives of the Poets.) What is meant by saying so? Did the English language "sink under him," as Addison says? (Spectator.) Or did he "form his style by a perverse and pedantic principle," so as to write "no language," but a "Babylonish dialect" "harsh and barbarous?" What is meant by "*no language?*" By "*Babylonish dialect?*" Is Milton's diction perspicuous to the unlearned? To any one? Is it lively? Suited to express the sublime? (Macaulay's Essay on Milton.) Are his diction and syntax suited to each other? To his subject? How so? Has his poetic diction been going obsolete since he published, or growing familiar? Has he added to the wealth of the English speech? New words? What? Phrases? What? Current quotations? What? Has he taught others to express elevated thought in sonorous diction? Can you mention great masters of English who have used him besides Burke and Webster? Write an essay on the language of Milton covering the ground of the foregoing questions!

SHAKESPEARE.

JULIUS CÆSAR.

PERSONS REPRESENTED.

JULIUS CÆSAR.
OCTAVIUS CÆSAR, MARCUS ANTONIUS, M. ÆMIL. LEPIDUS, } *Triumvirs after the death of Julius Cæsar.*
CICERO, PUBLIUS, POPILIUS LENA, *Senators.*
MARCUS BRUTUS, CASSIUS, CASCA, TREBONIUS, LIGARIUS, DECIUS BRUTUS, METELLUS CIMBER, CINNA, } *Conspirators against Julius Cæsar.*
FLAVIUS and MARULLUS, *Tribunes.*
ARTEMIDORUS, *a Sophist of Cnidos.*
A SOOTHSAYER.
CINNA, *a Poet.* *Another* POET.
LUCILIUS, TITINIUS, MESSÀLA, Young CATO, and VOLUMNIUS, *Friends to Brutus and Cassius.*
VARRO, CLITUS, CLAUDIUS, STRATO, LUCIUS, DARDANIUS, *Servants to Brutus.*
PINDARUS, *Servant to Cassius.*
CALPHURNIA, *Wife to Cæsar.*
PORTIA, *Wife to Brutus.*
SENATORS, CITIZENS, GUARDS, ATTENDANTS, etc.

SCENE, *during a great part of the Play, at Rome; afterward at Sardis; and near Philippi.*

INTRODUCTORY.—Write an account of the life and writings of Shakespeare; a life of Julius Cæsar, of Marcus Brutus; an outline of the narrative in the play of Julius Cæsar; an essay on Rome and the Romans during the times of Julius Cæsar.—(See Halliwell's or Hudson's Life of Shakespeare, Craik's English of Shakespeare, and Plutarch's Lives.)

Is Shakespeare known to have inherited his genius from his father or mother? Where was he born? What kind of place is Stratford geographically—*e. g.*, is it by any river, by the sea, by mountains, flat, hilly,

ACT I.

SCENE I.—*Rome. A Street. Enter* FLAVIUS, MARULLUS, *and a Rabble of* CITIZENS.

sandy, marshy, barren, fertile, quiet, stormy, the horizon near or remote, capable of what sunrises, sunsets, storm-scenes, and the like? What kind of place was it botanically—*e. g.*, how wooded, cultivated, how as to wild plants, flowers? What residences there or hard by—*e. g.*, town-houses, country-seats, castles? What literary opportunities—*e. g.*, libraries, schools teaching what? Why are these questions asked? Have they any thing to do with the development of Shakespeare's genius? How so? At what age did he leave Stratford? What is known of his life before that? What had occurred at Kenilworth to stimulate dramatic genius? What famous actors from the neighborhood? What did Shakespeare do in London? Who were his associates there? Mention important contemporary events! Did he know any thing of America? Com. of Errors, iii., 2: Raleigh. When did he begin to write for the public? What did he write? Was he gradually trained to the height of Hamlet and Lear, or did he write so from the first? Did he begin by revising the plays of others? Did he study hard? Write much? What besides plays? Did he re-write his own plays after trying them on the stage? What of the excellence of such training? How extensive was his acquaintance with the court? With the people? Was he in any sense a learned man? What did he learn—history of Greece, Rome, England, France? Any thing of law, medicine, theology, philosophy? Of languages and literature? Of men and manners? Was he in any sense one of the unlearned? In what sense? How far are his works original? How far do they embody his own character and experience? How far are they results of observation? How far are they characteristic of his age and country? What is the history of his fame? In what kind of composition is his fame greatest—tragic or comic, heroic or domestic, prose or poetry?

When was Julius Cæsar written? Was it probably a long time growing in the mind of Shakespeare? What lesson is it intended to teach? What conspiracies in England during the life of Shakespeare? On the Continent? What friends of Shakespeare connected with any of them? What in his relations to Elizabeth and James would add interest to the matter? Was it a subject to please the people? Is there evidence in

Flav. Hence; home, you idle creatures, get you home;

---

other plays that the story of Cæsar had long made a deep impression on his mind? Richard III., iii., 1; Hamlet, i., 1; iii., 2; v., 1; Cymbeline, iii., 1; Antony and Cleopatra, etc., etc. Study by aid of Clarke's Concordance! Could not a good drama be written closing with the assassination of Cæsar? Could it teach the same lesson as this play? Is the exhibition of the providential results of conspiracy an essential part of the action? Ulrici says that with Shakespeare the tragic element consists in the sufferings and final ruin of the humanly great, noble, and beautiful which has fallen a prey to human weakness; in whom does the interest of this tragic element center in this play? Is Cæsar or Brutus the hero? To what weakness does he fall a prey? Who is his tempter? Why is Portia introduced? Why Lucius? Antony? Why are the heroic elements of Cæsar's character kept so much out of view? Would they withdraw our sympathies from Brutus? Does Shakespeare's Brutus agree wholly with the Brutus of history? Explain any differences by reasons drawn from grounds of imaginative truthfulness, and unity of dramatic effect! Why are the Roman populace introduced? Does their character determine the futility of the conspiracy? How so? Has this play a proper beginning? Middle? End? A proper unity of action?—of time?—of place? Abundant variety in unity? Mention illustrations of variety! Show how it is combined into unity! What rank does this play hold among the works of Shakespeare?

(Write an analysis, filling up all the ellipses: see model in Appendix A. Study the grammatical etymology of pronouns, 214–244, and instinctive forms and pronominal elements, 305–309, in addition to the subjects referred to under Bunyan and Milton.)

Where does the scene open? When? (At the Lupercalia, 13th Feb., B.C. 44, after Cæsar was made dictator for life.) Who are there? Who speaks first? Who is Flavius?

What is the first clause? What ellipsis? 403, 380, X.; 396, XI. What kind of clause—declarative, interrogative, imperative, exclamatory, or optative? 404. What is the verb? 245. Subject, 380, VIII. What does *hence* combine with? Kind of combination? 407. Does it complete or extend the predicate? 408. Is it an adjunct of time, place, mode, or cause? 408. What language is it from? 296, II. Which is the root letter? 308, 6. Why called a pronominal element? 308, 6.

Is this a holiday? What! know you not,

What other words in English of the same pronominal element—pronouns? 229. Adverbs? 291, 296, II. Of what case does —*ce* represent the ending? 292. What other adverbs ending in —*ce?* 292, 296. II. How was this genitive ending written in Anglo-Saxon? 192. Was *hence* ever written *hennes, hens?* (Yes, Chaucer and others.) What relation of place is expressed by the genitive termination? 189, 396, VI. What grammatical equivalent for *hence?* 396, VI. Rule for the point after *hence?* 544. Rule for its capital? 564.

Next clause? (*home.*) What kind of clause? 404. Supply the ellipsis! 380, X. Verb? 245. Subject? 380, VIII. What part of speech is *home?* What word does it combine with? Kind of combination? 407. What noun is it derived from? From what case? 292. What preposition would express the relation? Does our idiom allow the use of *to* with it? Rule for the pause after *home?* 543.

Next clause? Does *you idle creatures* belong with any predicative combination? Why call it a quasi-proposition? Is it declarative, interrogative, imperative, exclamatory, or optative? 404. Parse *you!* 355, II. What kind of combination is *you+creatures?* 406. *Idle+creatures?* 406. What language is *you* from? 227. Which letter of it is a pronominal element? 308. In what cases was it in Anglo-Saxon? (Dative and accusative plural.) 227. In old English? (The same.) Is it ever used as a nominative in the Bible? What is the old nominative? 227. What English verb of the same root as *creature?* What grammatical equivalent for it containing the verb *create?* How comes it to be used as a term of contempt? Rule for the point after it? 543.

Next clause? Kind of clause? 404. Verb? 245. Subject? 380, VIII. Direct object? 374, VI. *Get+home* is what kind of combination? 407. Is this idiom in use now? What equivalent for it? In what respect is it analogous to *fare thee well?* Act iii., Scene 1; v., 3. *Get thee gone?* ii., 4. *I'll get me to a place?* ii., 4. Is *you* in its proper case according to derivation? Rule for point after this clause? 544.

Next clause? Kind of clause? 404. Direct or indirect interrogative? 404. Verb? 245. Subject? 174. Predicative combination? 405, 408. What is the sign of predication called in logic? 353. What language is *this* from? 236. What pronominal element has it? 308, 7. What other words of the same element, personal pronouns? Demonstrative? Adverbs? 296, 308. What is the natural significance of this

Being mechanical, you ought not walk,

---

element? 236, 308, 7. Equivalent to what gesture? What force has *a* compared with *one?* 216. What is the composition of *holiday?* Connection of thought between *holy day* and *holiday?* What point after this clause? Rule? 547. What capital? 564.

Next clause? How is *what* usually parsed in such cases? 376, XX., III. What kind of interjection? 305. Supply the ellipsis for a complete proposition to show how this use originated! What kind of clause have you made—declarative, interrogative, imperative, exclamatory, or optative? 404. What verb? Subject? What does *what* combine with? Kind of combination? What language is *what* from? 237. Which letters are the pronominal element? 308, 9. What is the natural significance of this element? 241, 308. What other words of the same element? Interrogative pronouns? Relatives? Adverbs of time?—place?—manner?—cause? 296, 308. What force has *—t* in *what?* (Neuter gender.) 237, 229.

Next clause? Kind of clause? 404. Verb? 245. Subject? 174. Rule for collocation? 356. *Know+not* is what kind of combination? 407. Which letter in *you* is the pronominal element? 308. What case is it in Anglo-Saxon? 227. In old English? In the Bible?

Next clause? Kind of clause? 409. Subordinate or co-ordinate? 411. Substantive, adjective, or adverb? 411. How governed? 411, I., 3. Verb? 245. Subject? 174. Is *you+being* a true combination, or is *being* merely a sign of the combination between *you* and *mechanical?* Expand *being mechanical* into a subordinate clause! What equivalent for *mechanical?* Is it now used in this sense? Does *not* combine with *ought* or *walk?* What kind of combination is *ought+walk?* 407, 408. In what mode is *walk?* Does it complete or extend the predicate? 408, 2, *e.* What preposition would express the relation between *ought* and *walk?* Is *to* now used for that purpose? What is the form of a verb called which is governed by a preposition in Anglo-Saxon? 263, 389. Is it as common as the other form? (No.) Why should it have become more common in English—is it an instance of a general analytic habit of the language? Unabr. Gram., 32. Give other examples of the use of prepositions now in place of old terminations! 193–195. Do the French use a preposition with the infinitive? Why should that affect the English? 41–43. Whence the form—*e. g., for to walk, What went ye out for to see,* Matth., xi., 8, 14; Acts, xvi., 4, 10? 388, I. (See

Upon a laboring day, without the sign
Of your profession? Speak, what trade art thou?

---

forward, Chaucer, verse 13.) Why should the form without *to* hold its ground longest in combinations with auxiliaries? 389. Are the phrases in most frequent use most stable? What connection of thought between *own, owe,* and *ought?* 242. To what auxiliaries is *ought* here analogous? 271, VII. *Upon* is a sign of what combination? What attributive combinations with day? Is *laboring* here the present participle? What is it? 313, 5, *a.* What analogy in its use here to *walking-stick, church-going bell, leather apron, captive bonds?* What equivalent for *laboring day* using a Norman genitive? 357. *Without* is the sign of what combination? What attributive combinations with *sign?* 406. What adjective equivalent to *of your profession?* What language is *the* from? What pronominal element in it? 308. Natural significance of this element? 236. Unabr. Gram., 167. What other words with the same element—demonstrative pronouns, personal pronouns, adverbs of time, of place, manner, cause? 308. What historic connection between *this, that,* and *the?* 217+. Is there a similar relation in other languages which have a definite article between it and the demonstrative? 218. Unabr. Gram., 287. What is meant by the following: *One* : *an* : : *that* : *the?* Does *the* give notice that *sign* is to be described, or has been described? Why is it called an article—connection of thought between this meaning of *article* and its other meanings? Which pronominal element has *your?* 308. What case is it in Anglo-Saxon? 227. What does *profession* mean here? Connection of thought between it and the verb *profess?* Any thing peculiar in the use of the word here? Why is *being mechanical* separated from the rest of the clause by a comma? Why is *upon a laboring day?* 543.

Next clause? To whom spoken? Why is this one singled out? Kind of clause? 404. Verb? 245. Subject? 352. Next clause? Kind of clause? Verb? 245. Subject? 380, VIII. Is *art* a copula? 353. What is the predicate? 353. What preposition might be used with *trade?* Could *of trade* be a predicate? 408. What of expressions like these: *A tapster is a good trade,* Merry Wives, i., 3; *Your hangman is a more penitent trade,* Measure for Measure, iv., 2? Is the ellipsis—*e. g.,* to be *a tapster* (=tapster-ing) *is a good trade,* or *a tapster is* of *a good trade?* In what form is the answer usually given to a question as to what a man's trade is? May the expected answer modify the form

1 *Cit.* Why, Sir, a carpenter.

---

of the question—*e. g.*, the expected answer being *a carpenter* instead of *carpentering* lead to saying *art thou* instead of *dost thou follow?* Does Shakespeare ever use *of* in phrases like this? (Once. Measure for Measure, ii., 1.) *What+trade* is what kind of combination? 406. Pronominal element in *what?* 308. Its natural significance? 241. Unabr. Gram., 167. Meaning of —*t* in *what?* 229. What other pronouns with the same ending? Pronominal letters in *thou?* 308. Their natural significance? 228. Other words of same element? What common idea in *thou* and *that?* Is pointing the finger a natural gesture to accompany both? Was *thou* used in the time of Shakespeare more than it is now? 228. From superiors to inferiors how? From equals to equals how? From inferiors to superiors? What illustrations of its use in 228? How is it that the same expression should in one case be a mark of contempt, in another of affection, in another of reverence? Do any class of persons now use it for *you?* What reason do they give for it? Was it ever a serious matter for them to say *thou* to a magistrate? Is *thou* used here with propriety? How so? Is this speech in verse? What kind? 493. The same as the Paradise Lost? 500. Does it sound like the Paradise Lost? Why not?

Scan the first verse! What kind of a foot is the first? 483. Where is the cæsura? 483. Scan the second! Cæsura where? Fourth foot what kind? Scan the third! Cæsura where? First foot what kind? Scan the fourth verse! Cæsura where? Third foot what kind? Scan the fifth verse! Cæsura where? Why after *profession* rather than *speak?* Does the tribune put his speech into meter, or does it come so?

Next clause? Who speaks? To whom? What does Worcester mean when he calls *why* a "mere emphatical expletive?" Is it the same word here as the common interrogative *why?* Supply an ellipsis so as to suggest how this use of *why* may have arisen! What kind of sentence? Verb? Subject? *Why* combines with what? What kind of combination? 407. Which letters in *why* are the pronominal element? 308. Natural significance of this element? 241. Other words of the same element? 308. What case is *why* in Anglo-Saxon? (Ablative. Unabr. Gram., 313.) Grammatical equivalent using *what?*

Next clause? (*Sir.*) A complete or quasi-clause? What kind? 404. How is *Sir* parsed? Next clause? Supply the ellipsis! Kind of clause? 404. Verb? 245. Subject? Predicate? 174.

Mar. Where is thy leather apron, and thy rule?
What dost thou with thy best apparel on?—

Next clause? Kind? Who speaks? To whom? Subject? 174. Is *is* a copula? 353. Predicate? 353. Is this either of the predicates enumerated in 353? Can not position be predicated as well as quality? Attributive combinations with *apron?* Grammatical equivalent for *leather apron?* What analogy with *laboring day?* What pronominal element in *where?* 308. Its natural significance? 241. Other words of the same element? What case is *where* in Anglo-Saxon? (Genitive and dative. Unabr. Gram., 313.) Grammatical equivalent for it using *what?* Pronominal element in *thy?* 308. Its natural significance? 228. Equivalent to what gesture? 228. Other words of same element? Why do Friends (Quakers) use *thou* for *you?* Why is it used here? What was the old English form of *apron?* (*Napron.*) What connection of thought between *n-apron* and *nap*, *napkin?* Should we print *leather apron* or *leather-apron?* Why? 555.

Next clause? Connective? Kind of clause? 404, 410. Verb? Subject? Copula? Predicate? Why ask for the apron and rule?

Next clause? Kind? 404. Verb? Subject? 352. Direct object? 360. *With* is the sign of what combination? Attributive combinations with *apparel?* 406. What part of speech is *on?* What ellipsis for it as a preposition? Is it the sign of an attributive or objective combination? 406, 407. What ellipsis for an objective combination, *worn* or *put?* Is *apparel+on thee* an allowable combination? What analogy between this use of *on* and that of *where* in the two last clauses? Do both describe the position of a thing rather than of an act—describe a substantive rather than a verb? Give other examples of this use of adverbs!

Next clause? To whom spoken? What has the carpenter done? Is this a true proposition? Of what kind—declarative, interrogative, imperative, exclamatory, or optative? 404. Is it a call for attention, or what ellipsis is there? Why is this citizen addressed as *you?* Is he a different kind of man from the first? What is *you* called when thus used? (*Pronomen reverentiæ.* Unabr. Gram., p. 561.) Why should it be considered courteous to say *you* rather than *thou?* What difference in the natural significance of *th* and *y?* 228. In what ways do other languages avoid the use of the demonstrative letters in courteous address? 230, 228.

You, Sir; what trade are you?
  2 *Cit.* Truly, Sir, in respect of a fine workman,
I am but, as you would say, a cobbler.

Next clause? How is *Sir* parsed? Does it couple naturally with *you?* Would *thou, Sir,* be good? Why not? Next clause? Kind of clause? Verb? In what number? Subject? 352. In what number? Do any grammars call *you are* singular? 228, 275. Why? Does the reason hold good for Shakespeare's language? Should *we* be put as a singular for a similar reason? 226. Is it true that *you are, we are,* are in any case destitute of all suggestions or associations of plurality? 226. If so, why does any one say *we* for *I?* Is *you* still a *pronomen reverentiæ?* Which is it that is different, the logical or the rhetorical force? What is the predicate of this clause? 353, 408. How is *trade* parsed? Pronominal letters in *what?* 308. Their natural significance? 241. Force of *—t?* 229. Other pronouns of same ending? Is this clause in rhetorical agreement with the first of the verse? Does this tribune talk prose? Scan the verses! Rule for the pause after *apron?* after *you?* after *Sir?*

Next clause? Who speaks? To whom? Does *truly* modify *am,* or, *e.g., speak* understood?—*to speak,* or *I speak?* Is it usual for inferiors to preface their speech with some affirmation like the cobbler's "Truly, Sir;" "Indeed, Sir?" Illustrate from the speech of the Irish—the negro! Of what natural feeling is it the expression? What relation has it to conversational oaths? Is it complimentary to a person to feel as if on oath when addressing him? Which kind of clause does *Sir* resemble? 404. What word is it contracted for?

Read the clause in which *am* is the verb! Its subject? Predicate? *A+cobbler* is what kind of combination? What rhetorical figure in *I am a cobbler?* 462. What are the two meanings? Why should *cobbler* (=*mender of shoes*) come to mean *clumsy workman?* What grammatical equivalent for *but?* What is the original full form for which *I am but a cobbler* is an ellipsis? What part of speech is Anglo-Saxon *butan* (=*but*)? (Preposition and conjunction.) Does *but* combine with *am* or *cobbler?* Kind of combination? Grammatical equivalent for *in respect of?* How can it mean *in comparison with?* What combination is *in* a sign of? What combination is *of* a sign of? What kind of combination is *respect+of workman?* How may *in respect of* be parsed togeth-

Mar. But, what trade art thou? Answer me directly.

---

er? 299, 7. As a sign of what combination? What difference between *with respect to* and *in respect of?* What attributive combinations with *workman?* Does *fine* literally describe the *workman* or the article wrought? By what figure is it applied to the *workman?* 459. What other words besides *a* from the Anglo-Saxon *ân?* Does the *a* with *workman* mean the same as the *a* with *cobbler?* Which is nearer the meaning, *one workman* or *any workman?*—*one cobbler* or *any cobbler?* What is the pronominal element in *I?* 308. Is *I* a substitute for a descriptive name (noun), or a direct designation of a person? 222. What propriety in calling it a pro-noun? Which is the more frequent designation of one's self, *I* or *me?* Do children use one for the other? What is the —*m* in *am?* 251, 3.

What other clause in this speech? What kind of clause—subordinate or co-ordinate? 409. Substantive, adjective, or adverb? 411. It modifies what? Connective? Verb? Subject? Any objective combination? 407. Mode and tense of verb? Analyze *would say;* parse *would* alone; *say* alone! Is *so to speak* a grammatical equivalent for this clause? What does the clause imply as to the use of the word *cobbler?* How so? What number is *you?* Why used here in addressing a single person? 228. Does this citizen talk in iambics?—in any meter? Rule for the comma after *truly?*—after *Sir?*—after *workman?* —after *but?*—after *say?* 543.

Next clause? Who speaks? To whom? What kind of clause does *but* indicate—subordinate or co-ordinate? 409. Copulative, disjunctive, adversative, or causal? 410. What are the two clauses it connects? Read the whole ellipsis!

Next clause? What kind in relation to the clause supplied after *but?* 411. Is it a direct object of *ask* understood? Verb? Subject? Predicate? Parse *trade!* Pronominal letters in *what?* 308. Force of —*t?* 229. Is —*t* in *art* a pronominal letter? Which pronoun does it represent? 251, 4; 308, 4. Pronominal elements in *thou?* 308. What is indicated by the use of *thou* here instead of the former *you?* What gesture naturally goes with *thou?* 228. Should there be a comma after *but?* Rule? 543.

Next clause? Kind of clause? 404. Verb? Subject? 380, VIII. What objective combinations? 407. Does *answer*+*me* complete or ex-

2 *Cit.* A trade, Sir, that, I hope, I may use with a safe conscience; which is, indeed, Sir, a mender of bad soles.

---

tend the predicate? 408. *Answer+directly?* Is *directly* an adjunct of time or manner? Connection of thought between *answer* and *swear?* Pronominal letter in *me?* 308. Other words of same element? What does the tribune understand to have been meant by *cobbler?* Does he speak in meter? Scan the line! Name the feet! What is —*ly* metrically? What is meant by *hypercatalectic?* Are such verses common?

Next clause? Who speaks? To whom? Kind of clause? 404. Verb? Subject? Predicate? Parse *trade!* What kind of combination is *a+trade?* 406. Next clause? Is *Sir* connected with any predicative combination? How is it parsed? Next clause? Subordinate or co-ordinate? Substantive, adjective, or adverb? It describes what noun? Connective? 237. Verb? Subject? Direct object? 360. What combination is *with* a sign of? What attributive combinations with *conscience?* Is not this clause a direct object of *hope?* Can the same clause be both a substantive and an adjective? Must every substantive clause containing a relative be so? Give examples! What pronominal element in *that?* 308. Its primary meaning? 236. Connection between *that* here and the demonstrative *that?* Force of —*t?* 229. What was the pronominal consonant of *I?* 308. Mode and tense of *may use?* Analyze it; parse *may* alone; *use* alone; give grammatical equivalents to illustrate that *use* is an infinitive!

What kind of clause is *I hope*, independent, subordinate, or co-ordinate? Is it part of the description of *trade?* What peculiarity in its relations to the clause in which *may use* is the verb? Connection of thought between *science* and *con-science?* What does the *con-* mean? 326, 8.

Next clause? Kind of clause—subordinate or co-ordinate? Substantive, adjective, or adverb? 411. What noun does it describe? Connective? 237. Verb? Subject? Predicate? Is *which+is mender* correct grammar? With what rule does it conflict? Can you supply an ellipsis so as to make good syntax? Did Shakespeare mean *which is to be a mender?* Whence the confusion? (Compare former text and questions.) What attributive combinations with *mender?* — with *soles?* What rhetorical figure in this clause? 462. What are the two mean-

Flav. What trade, thou knave? thou naughty knave, what trade?

---

ings of the sounds represented by *soles?* Difference between *mend* and *amend? Mender of souls* means what? Does the tribune understand him to mean *souls* or *soles?* What "menders of souls" were becoming objects of popular ridicule in Shakespeare's time? Was the Puritan a common character in comic plays a little later? What peculiarities of speech, dress, and manner were given him?—the same which are described in Hudibras?—the same which are now given in England to the traditional Yankee? Is this speech to be spoken with a sanctimonious snuffle? Would not that be an anachronism? Is there any natural connection between sanctimoniousness and snuffling? What historical connection?

How is *indeed* parsed? What etymological connection has it with the verb *do?* Which is more like it *in fact* or *in truth? Sir* is a quasi-clause of what kind? 404.

Next clause? Who speaks? To whom? Kind of clause? 404. Verb? Subject? Predicate? 353. Next clause? Is there a predicative combination with *thou?* 405—with *knave?* What kind of combination is *thou+knave?* 406. Next clause? Is *thou naughty knave* a true proposition? 174. Parse *thou!* What kind of combination is *thou+knave?—naughty+knave?* 406. Connection of thought between *naughty* and *naught*—what lines from Dr. Watts illustrate it? Is *knave* in any other place in the play? (Twice in Act iv., Scene 3; Brutus to Lucius:

"Poor knave, I blame thee not;"—
—"Gentle knave, good-night."

Connection of thought between the meanings of *knave?* Next clause? Predicative combination? 405.

Next clause? Who speaks? To whom? Parse *nay!* Will it enter into combination in a simple sentence? 396, IX. What kind of proposition is it like—declarative, interrogative, imperative, exclamatory, or optative? 404. For what proposition is it a grammatical equivalent? 396, IX. Etymological relation between *ay* and *nay?—nay* and *no?*

Next clause? Kind? 404. Verb? Predicative combination? 405. Objective combination? 407. Pronominal letter in *you?* 308. How related in force to *th?* 228. Is *you* here the *pronomen reverentiæ?* Con-

2 *Cit.* Nay, I beseech, Sir, be not out with me: yet, if you be out, Sir, I can mend you.

Mar. What meanest thou by that? Mend me, thou saucy fellow?

---

nection of thought between *seek* and *be-seech?* Force of *be-?* 315, 2. What kind of clause does *Sir* resemble? 404.

Next clause? Kind? 404. Verb? Subject? 380, VIII. What kind of combination is *be+out?* 407.—*be+not?* What combination is *with* the sign of? Meaning of *out with me?*—*out* of what?

Next clause? Kind of clause—copulative, adversative, disjunctive, causal? 410. Connective? What clauses are connected? Verb? Mode and tense? Analyze *can mend;* parse *can* alone; *mend* alone! Give grammatical equivalents for each! 272, 389. Predicative combination? 405. Objective combination? 407.

Next clause? Connective? Kind of clause? 411. Protasis or apodosis? 411, III., 4. What does it modify as an adverb? Subject? Predicate? Mode and tense of *be?* Why not *are?* Parse *Sir!* Connection of thought between *Sir* and *Senior?* Is the punning kept up? 462. What are the two meanings of *be out?* *Out* of what in each case? What does *mend you* mean from the *mender of souls?*—from the *mender of soles?* Which way does the tribune take him? What rhetorical form in a cobbler's *mend you?* 459, 469.

Next clause? Who speaks? To whom? Kind of clause? 404. Verb? Subject? Rule for collocation? 384, 7. Object? 360. What combination is *by* the sign of? Pronominal letters in *what?* 308. Their meaning? 241. Other words of same element—interrogatives, relatives, adverbs of time, place, manner, cause? Pronominal element in *thou?* 308. Its meaning? 228. In *that?* 308. Its meaning? 236. Other words of this element—personal pronouns, relative, adverbs, conjunction? Is *thou* rightly used? Why not call him *you*, as at first?

Next clause? Kind? 404. Verb? Subject? 352. Object? 360. Supply ellipsis to explain the tribune's state of mind!

Next clause? What syntactical combinations in *thou saucy fellow?* What kind of clause does it resemble—declarative, interrogative, imperative, exclamatory, or optative? 404. Pronominal letters in *thou?* Equivalent to what gesture? 228. Connection of thought between *sau-*

2 *Cit.* Why, Sir, cobble you.

Flav. Thou art a cobbler, art thou?

2 *Cit.* Truly, Sir, all that I live by is with the awl: I meddle with no tradesman's matters, nor women's matters, but, withal, I am, indeed, Sir, a surgeon to old shoes; when they are in great

---

cy and *sauce?*—*sauce* and *salt?* What is Attic salt? Is this regular meter? Coleridge reads,

"What mean'st by that?" etc.—

what need of such a change? Does not the sense show that the speech on page 48 belongs to the same tribune who speaks on page 49? Is it certain which it is? What reason for giving both speeches to Marullus?

Next clause? Who speaks? To whom? What ellipsis with *why?* Pronominal letters in *why?* From which case in Anglo-Saxon? (Ablative. Unabr. Gram., 313.) Other words of same element? 291. How is *Sir* parsed? Next clause? Verb? Subject? Object? Is *you* singular or plural? 228. *Cobble you* means what here? What rhetorical form? 459, 469.

Who speaks next? To whom? First clause? Subject? Predicate? Next clause? Subject? Predicate? What rule for collocation? 384, 7. Why say *thou?* Is this regular meter?

Who speaks next? To whom? What does *truly* modify? Subject of *is?* Predicate? What kind of clause is *that I live by?* It describes what? Meaning of the sentence? Read the clause in which *meddle* is the verb! What does it mean? Connection of thought between *meddle* and *medley?* Read the clause after *nor!* What verbal foolery? (2d Folio reads "woman's.")

What pun in *withal?* When it is understood to be *with awl*, what is the clause after *but?* What point after *awl* in that case? 546. What other change in the pointing? What is the clause after *but* when the next word is *withal?* Any reason for changing the reading here (the 1st Folio) to *with awl* or to *with all?* Which of the two meanings of any word in a pun should be represented to the eye? Any principle that decides this case? What kind of combination is *surgeon + to shoes?* What rhetorical form? 458, 452. What is the old form of *surgeon?* What analogy between *chirurgeon* and *handiwork?* Do you suppose

danger, I recover them. As proper men as ever trod upon neat's-leather, have gone upon my handiwork.

Flav. But wherefore art not in thy shop to-day? Why dost thou lead these men about the streets?

2 *Cit.* Truly, Sir, to wear out their shoes, to get myself into more work. But, indeed, Sir,

---

Shakespeare thought of this, and hence said *surgeon of old shoes?* What is the clause after *when?* The next one? Which is the leading clause? What does *recover* mean in surgeon's speech?—in cobbler's? What kind of clause is *as ever trod upon neat's-leather?* 411, III; Becker, 337. As an adverb what does it modify? What two clauses is this clause an abridgment of? Is the latter member of a comparison often abridged after *as?* Give examples! 401. What is this clause a circumlocution for? Is it well put in the mouth of this speaker? How so? What is the subject of *trod?* Should not *upon* be *down on?* Do English or Americans now use *upon* most frequently? Meaning of *proper men?* Hebrews, xi., 23.

Who speaks next? To whom? What two clauses are connected by *but?* (Compare second speech of Marullus.) Clause after *wherefore?* Grammatical equivalent for *wherefore* containing *what?* Meaning of *to* in *to-day?* Analogous uses of the preposition *to?*

Next clause? Kind of clause? 404. Verb? Subject? Direct object? What pronominal letters in *why?* 308. Grammatical equivalent containing *what?* How is *lead* parsed separate from *dost?* What pronoun does —*st* in *dost* represent? 251, 4. Force of pronominal element *th* in *thou?* 228—in *these?*—in *the?* Singular of *these?* Is —*e* the plural adjective ending in Anglo-Saxon? 236, 2. Does this speech suggest why this citizen was at first addressed as *you?*

Who speaks next? Does his *truly, Sir,* introduce more foolery? Clause with *truly?* How is *Sir* parsed? What ellipsis before *to wear?* Meaning of *out?* Connection of thought between *out* here and in *out of doors?* Did the Romans wear shoes like ours? Pronominal element in *their?* 308. Is *to get* in a separate clause from *to wear?* Composition of *myself?* Do the other personal pronouns take the genitive with *self?* 232+. Did you ever hear *his-self?* Was it ever in good

we make holiday to see Cæsar, and to rejoice in his triumph.

Mar. Wherefore rejoice? What conquest brings he home?

---

use? 233. Is the history of many "vulgarisms" similar? Give examples! What combination is *into* the sign of? What verbal antithesis here? 438. *More work* than what? Meaning of *get into more work?* Is there truth in this answer of the cobbler? What class of men are most forward now in getting up holidays? If tavern-keepers, why?

What clauses does *but* connect? (See before.) *Indeed* modifies what? Is it more like *in truth* or *in fact?* Pronominal element in *we?* Other words of same element? 308. Can there be a true plural of *I?* (Bopp, Comp. Gram., § 331.) Does *we* here mean *I and you*, or *I and they?* Do any languages have two forms to express these two meanings? Connection of thought between *holiday* and *holy day?* Meaning of *to* before *see?* 388, II. What does *and* connect? Pronominal element in *his?* 308. Other words of same element, what three adverbs of place? Meaning of *—s* in *his?* Describe a Roman general's *triumph!* Did Cæsar have a triumph for his defeat of Pompey's sons at Munda, Spain, 17th March, B.C. 45? (Yes, his fifth and last.) Is that what is meant here? Is there verisimilitude in making the cobbler a brawler and punster? How old is the proverb, Let the cobbler stick to his last? Is cobbling more apt to produce this character than tailoring?—than watch-making or other sedentary trades? If so, why? Why should any of them produce it?

Who speaks next? To whom? First clause? Kind of clause? 404. Verb? 245. Subject? 174, 356. What objective combination? Composition of *wherefore?* Which case of *what* does *where* represent? (Genitive and dative, 296, 236.) Grammatical equivalent for *where-fore?* Pronominal element? 308. Other words of the same element? Is it a relative or interrogative element in Anglo-Saxon? 237, II.

Second clause? Kind of clause? 404. Direct or indirect? Verb? 245. Subject? 174. Rule for collocation? 356, 1. Direct object? 360. What other objective combination? Does *home* complete or extend the predicate? 408. What kind of adjunct is it—of time, place, mode, cause? 408. What preposition would express the relation of *brings* to *home?* Does our idiom allow the use of it with *home* alone?—with *his*

What tributaries follow him to Rome,
To grace in captive bonds his chariot wheels?
You blocks, you stones, you worse than senseless things!

---

home or *our home?* Parse *home!* Meaning of —*t* in *what?* 229. Meaning of *conquest* here?—of *brings home?* Did the Roman general have borne before his triumphal chariot the countries he had conquered? Pronominal element in *he?* 308. Have other words of the same element occurred in the play? Who is *he?*

Third clause? Kind of clause? 404. Verb? 245. Subject? 174. Direct object? 360. Objective adjunct of place? 408. Of purpose? 388, II. What grammatical equivalent will expand *to grace* into a predicative combination? Is *in* the sign of a combination between *grace* and *bonds*, or *tributaries* and *bonds?* What does *wheels* combine with? Kind of combination? Meaning of —*s* in *his?*—of —*m* in *him?* 229. What analogy between *captive bonds*, and *laboring day* (verse 4), and *chariot wheels?* How does *captive bonds* differ from *captives' bonds?*—*chariot wheels* from *chariot's wheels?* What custom is referred to? Does this speech display rhetorical art? 424. What is its purpose—to persuade the people to do what? 424.—to bring the minds of the people to the same state with the speaker's in what respect? 425. Does he begin in a skillful manner? How so—whose triumphal processions would these questions remind the people of? What had been the most brilliant triumph ever seen in Rome? What other triumphs had Pompey received? What tributaries had graced Pompey's chariot wheels? Cæsar had just conquered whom? Is there anadiplosis here? 435. Erotesis? 451. Is the speech in regular meter? What kind of foot is the first? 483. Cæsura where in the first verse?—in the second?—in the third? What is the effect of the regular movement of the cæsura toward the end of the lines? (Compare Milton: questions, p. 20.) What is the last foot? Rule for the comma after *Rome?* 543.

Next clause? What kind of combination is *you*+*blocks?* 406. *You* +*stones?* 406. *You*+*worse?* Is there any predicative combination in the line? Read its clause! What kind of clause? 410, III. Connective? 301. What does it connect? Verb after it? Subject? Predicate? 353. What ecphonesis here? 446. What metaphors? 458. Does rhetoric teach the orator to call his audience blocks and stones?

O, you hard hearts, you cruel men of Rome,
Knew you not Pompey? Many a time and oft

Does a discussion of the rhetorical art of a particular speech imply a consideration of the character of the speaker and of the audience, and of the circumstances of both? What in the relations of the tribunes to the people carries off such an address? Were the tribunes popular favorites?—chosen for any purpose which would make a gift for scolding a popular qualification? Had the people heard Marullus berate the patricians, and liked it? Do demagogues usually have this gift? Why? Do the populace like to be scolded sometimes? Why? Are good disciplinarians favorites? Why? What kind of looking man do you conceive this tribune to be—*e. g.*, large, small, loud, gentle, rapid, slow; of what temperament, eyes, nose, dress, manners? What effect does this line produce on the populace?

Next clause? 402. *O* is a quasi-proposition of what kind? 404. A natural expression of what feeling? 305. What difference between *O* and *Oh?* 305, 548. Next clause? Kind of clause? 404. Has it any predicative combination? 405. What combinations has it? What rhetorical figures? 446? 469? 459? 458? Next clause? What combinations? What rhetorical art in this verse? How does it follow up the effect of the verse before? Next clause? Kind? 404. Direct or indirect? Verb? 245. Subject? 352. Object? 360. Rule for collocation? 356. Rhetorical form? 451. What art? Have remembrances of Pompey been before excited? What effect has the utterance of his name? Give illustrations to show the power of a name—*e. g.*, in love, in hatred! Is this a question of doubt or appeal? Unabr. Gram., p. 484. It is pregnant with what affirmative proposition?

Next predicative combination? 405. How many times must it be repeated to fill out the propositions which are here abridged? Is *up* to be repeated with it? Is *many a time and oft?* *Your infants in your arms?* Any other adjuncts? Analyze *many a time;* what does *a* mean? Horne Tooke, p. 592, says it is a corruption of *of;* how would you go to work to find out whether he is right? Ought the grammars or the dictionaries to explain it, or both? Can you find it explained in either? Failing there, where will you go next—to the Anglo-Saxon? [In Anglo-Saxon there are two forms of *many*—a substantive and an adjective. The adjective is often used in the singular with a singular noun, in the same way as the German *manch* and Latin *multus*—i. e., *manig man*=

Have you climbed up to walls and battlements,
To towers and windows, yea, to chimney-tops,
Your infants in your arms, and there have sat

---

many a man. This use continues abundant in semi-Saxon (Layamon) and in the earliest English (Ormulum); it is not uncommon in Robert of Gloucester; in Chaucer it is rare, except *many oon* following a plural —*e. g.*, "With him ther wente knyghtes many oon."

Cant. Tales, 2120.

In the Bible, as at present printed, it is not found. "*Many's the good time*" (T. Jones, ii., 105) still survives. The same form with the article inserted is also common in semi-Saxon—*e. g.*, *moni ennes monnes bone=many a man's bane* (Lay., i., 322); in Chaucer it is the established form; later there is fluctuation—*e. g.*, *a many of men*, *many of men*, *a many sons* (Shakespeare): these last, however, are probably descendants or examples of the noun *many*, which was in common use down to Shakespeare's time, and still survives in the phrases *a great many*, *a good many*: 365, 9; 367, VII., 369.] Why has the article been introduced in this phrase? Is *a hundred men* in any respect analogous? Is *twenty-five dollars a hundred?* Is *four times a space?*—*double a distance?* 365. Parse *time!* parse *many!* Are there any other adjective pronouns which take the article between them and the substantive? 365. What does *and* before *oft* connect? Is *many a time and oft* elsewhere in Shakespeare? Merch. Ven., i., 3; 1 K. Hen. IV., i., 2: *many time and oft*, 2 K. Hen. VI., ii., 1. What rhetorical form? 473. Other phrases of emphatic tautology? (*forever and ever; again and again.*) Is *many and many a time* a grammatical equivalent? Which is more in use now? Which is more forcible? Why? Analyze *have climbed;* parse *climbed* separately; what does it agree with as a participle? What is the complete proposition for which *and battlements* stands?—for which *to towers* stands?—*and windows?* What kind of quasi-proposition is *yea?* 396, IX., 404. Is a whole proposition implied? If so, give it! Proposition for which *to chimney-tops* is abridged? Reason for attaching *your infants in your arms* only to the last proposition? Does it in that way better cap the climax? 444. Are not these traits taken from the habit of a London populace? How did the Roman sovereign people provide for their convenience on such occasions? Is this an anachronism? What rhetorical art here? Main purpose of speech is what?

The live-long day, with patient expectation,
To see great Pompey pass the streets of Rome:

Immediate purpose here? For what secondary purpose does he wish to vividly depict one of Pompey's triumphs? To put them in the same state of mind that they were then in? How will that help to the main purpose? Is it a skillful way of exciting them against Cæsar to revive their old love for Pompey? Why better than a direct attack on Cæsar? What rhetorical maxim can you generalize from this? Why is the description of a triumph a skillful way of reviving love for Pompey? Can you generalize a maxim from it? Are the circumstances and the words skillfully picked and arranged to this end? How so? Why *your infants in your arms?* Is it specially vivid pictorially? How so? Vivid to the feelings? How so? Can you generalize? Would it not be better to have given a formal description—*e. g., Remember how Rome looked when Pompey triumphed; throngs of people climbed the walls,* etc., etc.? Write out such a description! Why is the tribune's way of putting it better?

Connection of thought between *window* and *wind?* What does it suggest about the Anglo-Saxon houses? *Chimney* is from the Latin: what does that suggest about the Anglo-Saxon houses—that they had no chimneys? *Infant* is from the Latin: what does that suggest—that the Anglo-Saxons had no *infants?* Syntax of *infants?*

Next clause? Kind of clause? Subordinate or co-ordinate? 409. Copulative, adversative, disjunctive, or causal? 410. Connective? *And* connects what clauses? Verb in this clause? 245. Subject? 352. Objective adjunct of place? 408—of time?—of manner?—of purpose? 388, II. Logical object of *see?* Subject of *pass?* Case of *Pompey?* Expand the last line into two complete propositions! What kind of combination is *pass+streets?* What is meant by it? Give illustrations of our use of *pass* with a direct object of place! Is our use like this? Which pronominal element is in *there?* 308. Grammatical equivalent for *there* containing *that?* Pronominal element in *the?* 308. What relation has *the* to *that?* 217. Is the article a part of speech essential to language? 218. What cultivated languages have none? 218. Is the origin of articles uniform? 218. Composition of *live-long?* Does it belong to any class of compounds described in the grammar? 316+. [The German has *den lieben langen tag=the lief* (dear) *long day.*] How is *day* parsed? What preposition would express the relation? What

And, when you saw his chariot but appear,
Have you not made an universal shout,
That Tiber trembled underneath her banks,

---

language is *streets* from? 37. What fact about the Roman roads does the history of this word suggest? Are they still to be seen in England? What rhetorical art in this clause? What is the state of mind of the people when it begins?—when it ends? Explain the effect!

Next clause? Kind of clause? 410. Connective? 410. It connects what clauses? Verb? 245. Subject? 352. Direct object? 360. Analyze *have made;* parse *have* alone; *made* alone! 272. Is *made* a weak or strong verb? 247. It is contracted from what? What pronominal element in *you?* 308. *You* was originally in what case? 227. Why *an* rather than *a?* Does it follow the rule in 216? Which is the original form? How late is the complete establishment of the rule? (Angus says printers are still apt to insert *an* before vocal *h* and *u.*—*Hand-Book; London*, 1862.) Connection of thought between *shout* and *shoot?* Read the clause after *when!* Kind of clause? 411. What kind of adverb? 411, III. Modifies what verb? Connective? 396, IV. Verb? Subject? Adjunct of time? 408. Logical direct object? Expand *appear* into a full clause! What is its subject? Parse *chariot!* Why is the subject of an infinitive put in the accusative? Is it usually, when expressed, in the position of an object of the verb on which the infinitive depends? 388, VII. Is the statement in 388, VII., correct throughout? Grammatical equivalent for *but?* What does *but* combine with? Meaning of the combination? Describe a triumphal chariot; how shaped; how drawn!—the dress of the conqueror! What kind of looking man was Pompey—good for such an occasion? Pronominal element in *when?* 308. Which case in Anglo-Saxon is *when* from? (Accusative.) What adverbs of place from the same element?—of time?—of cause?—of manner? Pronominal element of *his?* 308. Meaning of *—s* in *his?* Connection of thought between *chariot* and *cart?*—*cart* and *car?*—*car* and *carry?* What does the present meaning of *cart* suggest as to the use of wheeled vehicles among the early English? How may it suggest *street* and the questions asked about it before? Do you know the story of Sir Lancelot of the Round Table, especially why he was called Lancelot of the Cart?

Next clause? What other particle is understood before *that?* What

To hear the replication of your sounds
Made in her concave shores?

---

kind of clause? Subordinate or co-ordinate? 409. Substantive, adjective, or adverbial? 411. What does it modify? Its verb? *Tremble* is from Latin *tremulus* (=English *tremulous*); can you think of other examples of a euphonic *b* inserted after accented *m* followed by *l* or *r?* Any akin to *humility?*—to *numerous?* Subject? *Underneath* is a sign of what combination? *To* is a sign of what combination? What kind of combination is *trembled*+*to hear?* 407, 408. Does *to* have its usual meaning here—*i. e.*, purpose or end? Is *at* a common meaning of the Anglo-Saxon *to* before a gerund? 389. (Yes.) Grammatical equivalent for *to hear* using *at?* Expand *to hear* into a clause with full predicative combination! What is meant by *replication of sounds?* Do we now say *replication* or *reverberation?* Is *reverberation* in Shakespeare? (No.) Milton? (No. Cudworth has "*replications* [or echoes]," Chaucer has *reverberacioun*, so Bacon, Shakespeare has *reverb* and *reverberate*). Why say *her* banks, *her* shores? What rhetorical figure? 463. Was Tiber feminine in Latin? Are names of rivers usually so in Latin and Greek? Why does Shakespeare make it so? Is the *trembling* better suited to a woman? Would you not like to know, before you accept that explanation, whether he uses the same gender in other places? He does —why? Of what gender is *his* in Anglo-Saxon? 229.—in the Bible? Exod., xxxvii., 17; 1 Kings, vii., 23; Matt., v., 13; xxvi., 52.—in Shakespeare? Had *its* become fully established in the time of Milton? (No. He uses it perhaps only twice in Paradise Lost—i., 254; iv., 813. Trench says not at all—*English, Past and Present*, p. 120.) Did *his* of itself denote personification in Shakespeare's time? Is this a reason for frequency of feminine personification down to Milton? (Compare P. L., i., 723; ii., 4, 175, 271, 584, etc.) Are names of rivers usually feminine in the Germanic languages? (Yes, and in the Sclavonic: Grimm, D. G., 3, 386.) Why should these languages so differ from the Latin and Greek? Is it accident, or something different in the rivers or in the people? 181, 182; and see after: *Chaucer*, line 7.

Meaning of *concave shores?*—*concave* on account of a bend in the river, or the washing out of the banks into caves haunted by the River-goddess? If the first, why plural *shores?* Distinction between *shore* and *bank?* Is it the same here and in the next speech? Connection of thought between *shore* and *shear*, and *-share* and *-shire?* Between *bank* and *bankrupt?*

And do you now put on your best attire?
And do you now cull out a holiday?
And do you now strew flowers in his way,

What rhetorical art in the five last lines? The main end in the speech? The immediate purpose here? Rome at Pompey's triumph is here described in relation to which of the senses? In relation to which had it been before described? Is it the natural order of description—eye first, then ear? Why? Which affects most profoundly—*e. g.*, sight of pain without hearing, or hearing groans, etc., without seeing? Give illustrative facts! Are not the last verses rather grandiloquent? Are they suited to the audience? How so? Any peculiarities in the meter? Is the sound well suited to the sense? What words and phrases aid the effect most? Is

Made in her concave shores

a whole verse? Does Shakespeare often use hemistichs as lines? (Yes.) Why this one? Should there be a comma between *and* and *when?* Rule? 543. Should there be one after *banks?* Rule?

Next clause? Kind? 404. Direct or indirect interrogative? Is there any thing peculiar in the use of *and* here? Are there any co-ordinate sentences distinctly expressed?—or conceived? Is it used to enforce a contrast? Can you find this use described in your grammar? What are to be contrasted? State in full the train of thought, by implying which the contrast is enforced? Verb in this clause? Analyze *do put;* parse *do* alone; *put* alone! Give grammatical equivalents for each to show how *put* is governed! *Put your attire on* what?

Next clause? Kind? 404. Has *and* the same force as in the former line? What is the rhetorical purpose of the repetition? What is it called? 437. Analyze *do cull;* parse *do* alone; *cull* alone! Give grammatical equivalents for each! Connection of thought between *cull* and *collect? Cull out* from what? Connection of thought between *holiday* and *holy day?*

Next clause? Has *and* the same force as in the line before? Why is the anaphora continued? Verb? Analyze *do strew;* parse *do* alone; *strew* alone! Give grammatical equivalents for each! Subject? 352. Collocation? 384. Direct object? 360. What custom is referred to? Objective combination of time?—of place? Connection of thought between *flower* and *flour?* How late is the separation of these two words?

That comes in triumph over Pompey's blood?
Be gone!
Run to your houses, fall upon your knees,
Pray to the Gods to intermit the plague

(Johnson's Dictionary has *flower* with all the meanings; no *flour*.) Is this a common mode of reproduction among words? 340. Give other examples! What word generated from *antique?—human?—courtesy?* From what is generated *posy?—balm?—pity?* What propriety in calling this process fissiparous generation?

Next clause? Subordinate or co-ordinate? 409. Substantive, adjective, or adverbial? 411. Describes what noun or pronoun? Any thing unusual in the idiom? Grammatical equivalent for *that?* 237. Connective? 237. Verb? Predicative combination? 405. What combination is *in* a sign of? What word from *triumph* by "fissiparous generation?" What combination is *over* the sign of? *Pompey's+blood* is what kind of combination? 406. What rhetorical forms? 451. Climax? 444. Was the blood of Pompey shed at Munda? Does blood mean offspring here? If so, as its literal meaning or by special figure? Has the word rhetorical force for the tribune's purpose? How so? What art in saying *his, that comes in triumph over Pompey's blood*, instead of *Cæsar?* Should *his* have emphasis? What kind of foot is *his way?* How many syllables is *flowers* here? Rule for the comma after *way?* 543.

Next clause? Kind? 404. Verb? Subject? What does *gone* combine with? Parse it! How does this clause differ rhetorically from imperative *go?* Is this a complete verse? What fitness in such a bit of a hemistich here? Is there more propriety in having the pause indicated by the absent hemistich before or after *be gone?* Why? If before it, where should *be gone* be printed?

Next clause? Predicative combination? 405. What combination is *upon* the sign of? Are both parts (up-on) significant?

Next clause? Kind? 404. Predicative combination? 405. What combination is *to* the sign of? *Gods*, why plural? *Pray+to intermit* what kind of combination? 407. Expand *to intermit* into a clause with a predicative combination? Meaning of *intermit* here? How different from *withhold* in shade of idea and rhetorical force? Connection of thought between *plague* and *flog*;—who afflicts (=*flogs*) whom in a plague?

That needs must light on this ingratitude.
Flav. Go, go, good countrymen, and, for this fault,
Assemble all the poor men of your sort;

Next clause? Subordinate or co-ordinate? 409. Substantive, adjective, or adverbial? 411. Describes what? Connective? 376, I. Verb? Subject? 352. *Light+on ingratitude* is what kind of combination? 407. *Needs + must light?* Derivation of *needs?* 292. Grammatical equivalent using an analytic genitive? 194. Analyze *must light;* parse *must* alone; *light* alone! Give grammatical equivalents! What ingratitude were the people guilty of? Pronominal element in *that?* 308. Other words of same element? Meaning of —*t* in *that?* 229. Other words in which —*t* has same meaning? Meaning of —*s* in *needs?* 292. Pronominal element in *this?* 308. Natural significancy of it? It corresponds to what gesture? 228. What rhetorical art in this conclusion? What sentiments are appealed to? Does it give a climax with the foregoing? 444.

Who speaks next? To whom? First clause? Predicative combination? 405. Next clause? Predicative combination? 405. What rhetorical form? 450. Next clause? Has it a predicative combination? What kind of proposition is it most like? 404. Meaning of *countrymen?* Is *fellow-countrymen* good English? Meaning of *good* here? Give examples of its similar use! Matt., xx., 11. Does this tribune's manner differ from the other's? In what respect?

Next clause? Predicative combination? 405. Direct object? 360. Attributive combinations with *men?* 406. Does *the* here direct attention to its substantive as having been before described or as to be described? What words constitute the description? Meaning of *sort?* What combination is *for* the sign of? Pronominal element in *this?* 308. Natural significance? 228. Other words of same element; personal pronouns; adverbs of manner? Pronominal element in *the?* What is meant by *one : a : : that : the?* Pronominal element in *your?* 308. How related in natural significance to *th?* 228. Meaning of —*r* in *your?* 227, 225, 209. Other pronouns in which it has the same force? Connection of thought between *assemble* and *simul*-taneous? Is the *b* in *assemble* euphonic or emphatic? When is it inserted? (See before, p. 58.) Give other examples!

Draw them to Tiber banks, and weep your tears
Into the channel, till the lowest stream
Do kiss the most exalted shores of all.
[*Exeunt* CITIZENS.

Next clause? Predicative combination? 405. Objective combinations? 407. Why not *Tiber's banks?* Pronominal element in *them?* Is *them* a personal pronoun in Anglo-Saxon? 229. Force of —*m?* 229. Give other words in which it is a sign of the dative case! Why has the dative termination rather than the accusative survived for our objective? Connection of thought between *bank* and *bankrupt?*

Next clause? Kind of clause? 404, 409. Verb? Subject? 380, VIII. Objective combinations? 407. Is *tears* a direct or factitive object? 360. What fitness in calling it a cognate accusative? Is it not pleonastic? 473. Connection of thought between *weep* and *whoop?* What does it suggest about the manners of early ages? Is *weep tears* a common idiom in Shakespeare? (No; *shed tears,* or *drop.*)—in the English Bible?—in Milton? (Yes; never *shed,* once *drop some tears.*) What characteristic of Milton is indicated? Connection of thought between *channel* and *canal?*—and *kennel?*—and *cane?*—and *cannon?*—and *canon?* Any fissiparous generation here? *Your tears*—has *you* the same meaning here as before? Does *the* direct attention to its substantive as well known, or to be described? Is this the use described in 370, X.?

Next clause? Kind of clause? 411. It modifies what? Its verb? Subject? Object? What is meant by *lowest stream?*—*most exalted shores?* Rule for the formation of superlatives? 202+. Which is the Anglo-Saxon mode of formation? Why should short words form in the Anglo-Saxon way more than long ones? Any other reason than that given in 203? *Of all* what? What relation is denoted by *of?* 359. Why called partitive? Connection of thought between *shore* and *shear?* Difference between *shore* and *bank?* Ought not the verb to be *does kiss?* Meaning of *kiss?* What figure? 463. Is the tribune in earnest in the substance of this direction? Do you know any custom which would countenance such a performance? What is hyperbole? 458. Is this mighty pathetic? Does it answer its purpose? Is it, therefore, true eloquence?

Next clause? To whom spoken? Predicative combination? 405, 380, VIII. Next clause? Kind of clause? 409. Should not the verb

See, whe'r their basest metal be not moved!
They vanish tongue-tied in their guiltiness.
Go you down that way towards the Capitol;
This way will I: Disrobe the images,
If you do find them deckt with ceremonies.

---

be *is moved?* Was the use of *whether* as one syllable common in the time of Shakespeare? (Yes, printed exactly like the adverb *where.*) Connection of thought between *metal* and *mettle?* Which is meant here? The metaphor is taken from the metal of what? How late is the adoption of the form *mettle?* (It is in Bailey's Dictionary.) Is it a case of fissiparous generation? What other cases have occurred in this extract? Is *basest* here a partitive or general appellative? Translate the clause into other language! Is this the real opinion which demagogues hold of the people they manage?

Next clause? Predicative combination? 405. Meaning of *vanish?* It suggests a comparison between what? It sounds like what cant word that might be used for it? What interest has the last question for the scientific linguist? Meaning of *tongue-tied?* Whence the word?—is the tongue ever literally tied? Pronominal element in *they?* 308. Meaning of it? Was *they* a demonstrative in Anglo-Saxon? 229. Meaning of *—r* in *their?* 229, 209.

Next clause? Predicative combination? 405. Parse *way!* How is it known what way he means? The pronominal element in *that?* 308. What gesture is it equivalent to? How does Shakespeare pronounce *towards?* How can you tell? What part of the city could they have been in, so that going to the Capitol would be *down?* Force of *the?* 370. Difference between *Capital* and *Capitol?* Are these words produced by fissiparous generation? What ellipsis in the next clause? 403. Pronominal element in *this?*—in *I?* What kind of clause is *disrobe the images?* How does *dis-* affect the meaning of *robe?* 326. Should it not rather be *derobe?* Give other words in which *dis-* has the same sense! What *images* are meant? What is meant by *disrobing* them?

Next clause? Protasis or apodosis? 411. Verb? Subject? Direct object? Analyze *do find;* parse *do* alone; *find* alone. Give grammatical equivalents for both! What kind of form is *do find* called? 280. Is *do* really emphatic here? In such cases does it now strength-

Mar. May we do so?
You know, it is the feast of Lupercal.
Flav. It is no matter; let no images

---

en or enfeeble the expression? Is the unemphatic form common in Shakespeare? How many times has it occurred in this extract? Was it then an archaism? Do young poets often use it now? Why? Connection of thought between *deck* here and *deck* of a ship? Is *decorate* of the same root? Has it perhaps affected the meaning of *deck?* How? Meaning of *ceremonies?* [Insignia, *e. g.*, of royalty or the like.—"His (a king's) ceremonies laid by, in his nakedness he appears but a man," K. Hen. V., iv., 1.—"There were set up images of Cæsar in the city, with diadems upon their heads like kings. These the tribunes, Flavius and Marullus, went and pulled down," North's Plutarch.] Connection of thought between the common meaning of *ceremonies* and this? (Compare

—"and th' invisible
Glory of him that made them, to transform
Oft to the Image of a Brute, adorn'd
With gay *Religions* full of Pomp and Gold,—etc."
P. L., i., 369+.)

Rule for the point after *moved?* 548. After *Capitol?* 544. After *I?* 545. After *images?* 543. Does this tribune speak in iambics? Good ones? With more or less variety than the former?

Who speaks next? To whom? Verb? 245. Subject? 352. *Do+so* is what kind of combination? 407. Analyze *may do*; parse *may* alone; *do* alone! 272, 389. Is this the common use of *do?* *Do so* represents what clause?

Next clause? Government of *it is the feast of Lupercal?* 411, I., 3. What does *it* stand for? 373, XIII. Predicative combination? 405. When was the feast of Lupercal holden?—in honor of whom? Why so called? How does Shakespeare pronounce Lupercal? How do you find out? With what ceremonies was it holden? How do you reconcile this statement with the second line in the scene?

Who speaks next? First predicative combination? 405. Connection of thought between the common meaning of *matter* and the meaning here?—between *matter* and *material?* Old form of *it?* 229. What is the pronominal letter in *hit?* 308. Force of *—t* in *it?* 229. It is the neuter of what masculine?

Be hung with Cæsar's trophies. I'll about,
And drive away the vulgar from the streets:
So do you too, where you perceive them thick.
These growing feathers pluckt from Cæsar's wing,
Will make him fly an ordinary pitch;
Who else would soar above the view of men,
And keep us all in servile fearfulness. [*Exeunt.*

Next clause? Verb? Subject? 380, VIII. Syntax of *images?* *Be hung* combines with what? Kind of combination? 407, 408. Analyze *be hung;* parse *be* alone; *hung* alone! Can *let be hung* be parsed together? 271, VIII. (See Paradigms.) What kind of combination is *Cæsar's+trophies?* 406. Meaning of *trophies?*—same as *ceremonies* above? What kind of clause is *I'll about?* Its verb? 289, 380, X.

Next clause? Predicative combination? Mode and tense of verb? Analyze it! Connection of thought between *away* and *way?* Meaning of *the vulgar?* Connection of thought between this meaning and that in *vulgar fractions?* What questions have been asked about *street?*

Next clause? Verb? Subject? Does *do* represent a clause or belong with a verb understood? Next clause? Kind? 411. Verb? Subject? Object? Is *thick* an attributive adjective? Is it better called predicative or factitive? Why?

Next clause? Verb? Subject? What kind of combination is *make+him?*—*make+fly?*—*fly+pitch?* What attributive combinations with *feathers?* What figure in this clause? 458. Put it in the form of a simile! 467. There is a metaphor like this in the Letters of Junius, which has been called the best in our literature: do you remember it? 476, 12. If Junius had this passage in mind while writing, is he guilty of plagiarism? Meaning of —*e* in *these?* 236.—of —*m* in *him?* Why should the dative sign be kept for our objective? Is it so in other pronouns? Connection of thought between *pitch* and *pick?* Does *point* ever mean *pick?*—ever mean *pitch?* Give examples! Does *fly a pitch* mean *fly to a point on a scale?* Whence the phrase "stick a pin there?"

Next clause? Kind of clause? 411. Describes what? Is *him* emphatic? What difference would be made in the sense by giving emphasis to *him* and omitting the point after *pitch?* What connective and personal pronoun would be an equivalent for *who?* Is the addition in

SCENE II.—*The same. A public Place. Enter, in procession, with music,* CÆSAR; ANTONY, *for the course;* CALPHURNIA, PORTIA, DECIUS, CICERO, BRUTUS, CASSIUS, *and* CASCA, *a great crowd following, among them a* SOOTHSAYER.

* * * * * *

Sooth. Cæsar.
Cæs. Ha! who calls?
Casca. Bid every noise be still:—Peace yet again.
[*Music ceases.*
Cæs. Who is it in the press that calls on me?
I hear a tongue, shriller than all the music,
Cry, Cæsar. Speak; Cæsar is turned to hear.
Sooth. Beware the ides of March.
Cæs. What man is that?
Brut. A soothsayer, bids you beware the ides of March.
Cæs. Set him before me, let me see his face.

---

this way of a subordinate clause to a sentence which had been completed common in Shakespeare? (Yes.)—common in careful writers now? What effect on the style? Does it add to its air of ease and naturalness? Analyze *would soar!* What figure? 458. The literal meaning.

Next clause? Kind of clause? Mode and tense of the verb? Is the figure of the former line carried out? How is keeping in fearfulness connected with soaring out of view? Pronominal element in *us?* 308. Other words of same element? 225. (Go on with similar questions through the additional extracts!)

Synoptical.—Is this a good scene to open with? Why? What is there to attract attention—show, bustle, fun, eloquence? (Is the second scene a good one to follow? Why?)

What variety in this scene among the characters? Difference between the tribunes and the people? Between the tribunes? Between the carpenter and the cobbler? What variety in looks? Describe Marullus! (See above, p. 54.) Describe Flavius! Do you imagine him large or small?—loud or gentle?—of what temperament?—general shape and size of head?—phrenological bumps?—eyes, nose, mouth?—manners? Which tribune would use most Anglo-Saxon? Describe the

Cas. Fellow, come from the throng: look upon Cæsar.
Cæs. What say'st thou to me now? Speak once again.
Sooth. Beware the ides of March.
Cæs. He is a dreamer: let us leave him;—pass.
[*Sennet. Exeunt all but* BRUTUS *and* CASSIUS.

(*A dialogue follows, in which* CASSIUS *works* BRUTUS *against* CÆSAR.)

Re-enter CÆSAR *and his Train.*

* * * * * *

Cæs. Antonius.
Ant. Cæsar.
Cæs. Let me have men about me that are fat;
Sleek-headed men, and such as sleep o' nights:
Yond Cassius has a lean and hungry look;
He thinks too much; such men are dangerous.
Ant. Fear him not, Cæsar, he's not dangerous;
He is a noble Roman, and well given.

---

cobbler!—the carpenter! The dress of the tribunes?—of the people? (Similar questions about the characters in the second scene!)

What variety in the action? The people are doing what at the beginning of the scene? In the middle? At the end? What change in their feelings? (Similar questions about the second scene.)

What variety in the sentiments? Are there comic and tragic thoughts? Foolery and eloquence? The eloquence runs through what changes? (What additional variety in the second scene? What sentiment comes in with the soothsayer?)

What variety in the language? Prose and verse? Cobbler's puns and tribune's tropes? Is the attention of the audience wholly occupied with the scenic present? The speech of Marullus adds what variety in this respect? (Is the language of the second scene different from the first? What variety in it?)

What unity between the tribunes? Are they a pair with complementary qualities?—having a common purpose?—a common position? What unity between the tribunes and the people? Are they matched? Point out the qualities which couple! Are they members of one body? What is the fable of Menenius Agrippa? (Coriolanus, i., 1.) How

Cæs. Would he were fatter:—but I fear him not.
Yet if my name were liable to fear,
I do not know the man I should avoid
So soon as that spare Cassius. He reads much:
He is a great observer, and he looks
Quite through the deeds of men: he loves no plays,
As thou dost, Antony: he hears no music:
Seldom he smiles; and smiles in such a sort,
As if he mocked himself, and scorned his spirit
That could be moved to smile at any thing.
Such men as he be never at heart's ease,
Whiles they behold a greater than themselves;
And therefore are they very dangerous.
I rather tell thee what is to be feared,
Than what I fear; for always I am Cæsar.
Come on my right hand, for this ear is deaf,
And tell me truly what thou think'st of him.

---

many good pictures should the stage present during the scene? Should a photograph of it at any moment have unity in the grouping? Describe the central object and the grouping—*e. g.*, at the opening;—at "Mend me, thou saucy fellow!"—at "Know you not Pompey?"—at "Be gone!" Tell how each of the characters looks! (Similar questions about the second scene! Which part of the body politic is represented in it?)

Is there any unity between the comic and serious parts? In what do they have a common ground? Does the classic drama admit such contrasts? Does nature? Is it a good reason for using them that they are found in nature? Does art copy every thing in nature? To what is the ultimate appeal in questions about the nature of beauty? How is the blending of prose and verse to be justified? Are thought and expression intimately united in Shakespeare?

What is the main idea of the play? How does this scene contribute to its development? What art is shown in preparing the audience for coming scenes? Are the relations of Cæsar to the parties of Rome well brought out? Any thing which leads us to forebode a Brutus for Cæsar? What? What do we learn from this scene of the character of

THE MERCHANT OF VENICE.

ACT V. SCENE I.

(Reprint of first Folio. Bring it to good sense and meter by correcting punctuation, etc., and by conjectural emendation, if necessary.)

Lorenzo. How sweet the moone-light sleepes vpon this banke,
Ieere will we sit, and let the sounds of musicke
Creepe in our eares soft stilnes, and the night
Become the tutches of sweet harmonie:
Sit *Iessica*, looke how the floore of heauen
Is thicke inlayed with pattens of bright gold,
There's not the smallest orbe which thou beholdst
But in his motion like an Angell sings,
Still quiring to the young eyed Cherubins;
Such harmonie is in immortall soules,
But whilst this muddy vesture of decay

---

the Roman populace? Can it be generalized? What of the character of the Roman demagogue? Can it be generalized? How came Shakespeare by this knowledge of them? What rhetorical maxims for dealing with the populace may be deduced from the scene? In what proportions and in what order are scolding and cajoling to be mixed? What rhetorical forms come most into play?

How is the genius of Shakespeare shown in this scene? What in it is created according to nature? The characters? The grouping? The language? Is there any display of Shakespeare's personal character in the scene? Can it not be safely inferred from it that he was an admirer of Pompey?—that he was no admirer of "the vulgar?" Why not? Can we form conclusions from this scene as to the language of Shakespeare? Does not each character speak a language of his own? Should you not expect, *e. g.*, the proportion of Anglo-Saxon words to change with the characters?—the syntactical peculiarities also? Would you expect the language to change wholly, as much as if the speeches of one character were written by Shakespeare, and those of another by Walter Scott? Why so? Would the several speeches have peculiarities common to the age of each writer? How if speeches written by Shakespeare were compared with others written by Ben Jonson? Would

Doth grosly close in it, we cannot heare it:
Come hoe, and wake *Diana* with a hymne,
With sweetest tutches pearce your Mistresse eare,
And draw her home with musicke.
Iessica. I am neuer merry when I heare sweet musique.
Play musicke.
Lor. The reason is, your spirits are attentiue:
For doe but note a wilde and wanton heard
Or race of youthful and vnhandled colts,
Fetching mad bounds, bellowing and neighing loud,
Which is the hot condition of their bloud,
If they but heare perchance a trumpet sound,
Or any ayre of musicke touch their eares,

---

you expect to find peculiarities common to all Shakespeare's writing different from those of Jonson? Why so? What words in the speech of Marullus, p. 52+, are not from the Anglo-Saxon? (Rejoice, conquest, tributaries, Rome, grace, captive, chariot, *block?* sense, cruel, Pompey, battlements, chimney, infant, patient, expectation, pass, appear, universal, Tiber, trembled, replication, concave, put, attire, cull, flowers, triumph, pray, intermit, plague, ingratitude.) Why should you expect *conquest* to be from the Norman? 43. Which of the other words for the same reason? What is the ratio of the Romanic words to the whole number of words in the speech? Is it more or less than usual? (Bunyan, Milton, App. B.) Is the reason to be found in the matter or the speaker?

What words used by Flavius in his first and two last speeches are not Anglo-Saxon? (Creatures, mechanical, laboring, sign, profession, trade: country, fault, assemble, poor, sort, Tiber, channel, exalted, basest, metal, moved, vanish, capitol, disrobe, images, ceremonies: matter, Cæsar, trophies, vulgar, perceive, ordinary, soar, view, servile.) What is the ratio of these to the whole? Greater or less than Marullus uses? Which of these words can be classified with *conquest*, etc.? What reason for *mechanical* being Romanic? 43. Of what nation were the mechanics? What other words here Romanic for the same reason? What words of the cobbler's speech not Anglo-Saxon? (Sir, respect, fine, trade, use, safe, conscience, mender, mend, meddle, matters, surgeon, danger,

You shall perceiue them make a mutuall stand,
Their sauage eyes turn'd to a modest gaze,
By the sweet power of musicke: therefore the Poet
Did faine that *Orpheus* drew trees, stones, and floods.
Since naught so stockish, hard, and full of rage,
But musicke for time doth change his nature,
The man that hath no musicke in himselfe,
Nor is not moued with concord of sweet sounds,
Is fit for treasons, stratagems, and spoyles,
The motions of his spirit are dull as night,
And his affections da ke as *Erobus*,
Let no such man be trusted: marke the musicke.

---

recover, proper, Cæsar, rejoice, triumph.) Is the ratio greater than in the speeches of the tribunes? Explain why it is as it is!

How many adjective clauses in the speeches of Marullus? How many in those of Flavius? How many in the whole scene? How many substantive clauses? Interrogative? Exclamatory? What syntactical differences from Milton? (See p. 34.) Is Shakespeare more perspicuous? 470–472. More lively? 473, 474. Is this a good extract for drill on the pronouns? Which part of it best? What part do personal pronouns play in conversation as compared with essays and formal composition? How do they affect the liveliness of style? 222. Unabr. Gram., 291. (Similar questions to most of the foregoing should be put, to sum up the results of the study of the other extracts. Let the student be required to write out for himself a complete series of all the additional questions suggested on page 66 and onward.)

It is not without significance that the greatest and most sovereign poet of the new time, in distinction from the old classic poetry—I can, of course, only mean Shakespeare—had the English tongue for his foster-mother.—*J. Grimm.*

What is the significance of the above fact? Point out how his mother-tongue is the poet's foster-mother!

"We must be free or die who speak the tongue
That Shakespeare spake."

Why so? Why say Shakespeare rather than, *e. g.*, Milton or Bunyan? Whence the quotation?

Did Shakespeare make any new words? (Probably not.) Any new

Enter Portia and Nerrissa.

Por. That light we see is burning in my hall:
How farre that little candell throwes his beames,
So shines a good deed in a naughty world.
Ner. When the moone shone we did not see the candle?
Por. So doth the greater glory dim the lesse,
A substitute shines brightly as a King
Vntill a King be by, and then his state
Empties it selfe, as doth an inland brooke
Into the maine of waters: musique, harke. *Musicke.*
Ner. It is your musicke Madame of the house.
Por. Nothing is good I see without respect,
Methinkes it sounds much sweeter then by day?

---

etymological forms? (No.) Any new rules of syntax? (No.) Do not his gentlemen speak the most natural idiomatic English? Had any gentleman ever spoken exactly so? How does this ideal speech differ from the actual? Does it omit awkwardnesses, barbarisms, fashionable slang, infelicities of every kind?—and select from every side and combine felicitous phrases adapted to the genius of the language?—and make felicitous new combinations of familiar words, which sound as though any body might have said them? Does the cobbler speak an ideal cobbler's speech? How formed from the actual; by what omissions; by what additions? How great is the variety of phraseologies required for the characters of Shakespeare? Can you mention any kind of person that does not talk in his pages? Any art or science, or field of experience or thought the language of which is not used? Would you not expect, then, to find in Shakespeare all the words in the language? How many words are there in Shakespeare? (About fifteen thousand; one third or one fourth of those current in his time.) Is this economy of words characteristic of the greatest masters of language? How many words in Milton's poetry? (About eight thousand.) How do Shakespeare and Milton show their mastery of language? Is the creative power in all departments of art shown in a similar way? State how—*e. g.*, in painting; in oratory; in musical composition?

Is Shakespeare's power of creating musical combinations of sound as wonderful as his other powers? Does he use rhyme in any of his

Ner. Silence bestowes that vertue on it Madam.
Por. The Crow doth sing as sweetly as the Larke
When neither is attended: and I thinke
The Nightingale if she should sing by day
When euery Goose is cackling, would be thought
No better a Musitian then the Wren?
How many things by season, season'd are
To their right praise, and true perfection:
Peace, how the Moone sleepes with Endimion,
And would not be awak'd.

---

works? In which? Is he master of the effects to be produced by it? Does he cultivate alliteration? 491. (He ridicules the abuse of it—*e. g.*,

> "The prayfull Princesse pearst and prickt
> a prettie pleasing Pricket," etc.—*Love's L. Lost*, iv., 1.)

Is it natural to forcible description? Are descriptives beginning with the same sound likely to have something of the same sense? Why so? Does this give them power to double the impressiveness of an image? Are they naturally associated for any other reason? What? What alliteration on page 69?—on page 70?—71? What other repetition of similar sounds was fashionable in Shakespeare's time? (Euphuism: the bringing into correlation words of similar sound but different sense. See Sir Piercie Shafton, Scott's Monastery.) Does Shakespeare use it? (Sometimes, though he ridicules it—*e. g.*,

> "Some say a sore, but not a sore,
> till now made sore with shooting," etc.—*Love's L. Lost*, iv., 1.)

What example of it on page 73? Do the extracts above show that Shakespeare loved music?—and thought it bad not to love it? Any more than they show that he admired Pompey? (See page 69.) Why so? Does he much use any of the minor artifices of versifiers? Is onomatopœia abundant in his pages? 305. Do his thoughts seem to come to him in such form that their most natural expression is most truly musical? What part of the current happy harmonious phrases of our language are from Shakespeare? Which has the greater variety and ease in the harmony of his verse, Shakespeare or Milton? Which is the more wonderful, the human voice or an organ? Shakespeare or Milton? Write an essay on the language of Shakespeare covering the ground of the foregoing questions!

SPENSER.

THE FAERY QUEEN.

INTRODUCTORY.—Write a life of Spenser: an essay on the Elizabethan Age; the manners of the court and of the people; the condition of learning, literature, and religion; the nature and sources of the greatness of the age: an essay on the Faery Queen; its character, its relation to the age, its history.—(See Chambers's Cyclopædia of English Literature, Drake's Life and Times of Shakespeare, Motley's Rise of the Dutch Republic, Warton on Spenser, Hart's Essay on Spenser and the Fairy Queen.)

At which university did Spenser study? What were then the studies of the universities? Their usages? How long was he there? What did he do after graduating? What did he publish first? When? How came he to live in Ireland? Was his residence favorable to study and poetic composition? What were his favorite books? Did he write much? What did he publish? What is known of his person and manners? His friends? What mutual friends had he and Shakespeare? Did he write most for the people, or scholars, or the court? Which of his writings have a puritanic cast? Are any of them in the meters of the ancients?

When was the Faery Queen composed? What kind of a work is it? Give its plan as set forth by Spenser! Why is it called the Faery Queen? Is it complete? How mnch is there of it? Enough for most readers? What is an allegory? 432. Difference between allegory and fable? 440.—and metaphor? 458.—personification? 463.—parable? 460.—a myth? What is the Faery Queen in external form? Were romances of chivalry part of the favorite reading of the time? Mention any! Who were the most fashionable poets? Did Ariosto and Tasso write

A gentle knight was pricking on the plain,

---

romances of chivalry? Were the artificial manners and gallantries of chivalry still current in the court of Elizabeth? Were jousts and tournaments still the fashion? What is the Faery Queen in its internal sense? A book of religious training? Was Spenser accustomed to see the virtues and vices visibly decorated with their proper attributes, and speaking and acting representatively? What was a pageant? A masque? A dumb show? Was allegory used in these public spectacles? (Read Scott's Kenilworth and Motley's Rise of the Dutch Republic.) Do descriptions in the Faery Queen bear marks of being suggested by these allegorical figures? F. Q., 3, 12, 5+. Was the style of dress at court such as to make the varied and splendid costumes in the Faery Queen natural? Was the blending of chivalry and religious earnestness common in the times of Elizabeth? What other element of fashionable success had Spenser's book? Did the characters represent prominent persons? For example? What is the effect now of the double allegory? Is there any great work of chivalry, written as an allegory, which is more obscure than this? (See Tasso: Jerusalem Delivered.)

What other source of obscurity in the poem? Did Spenser use the current language of his time? What does Ben Jonson mean when he says that "Spenser, in affecting the ancients, writ no language?" Have other learned poets been fond of the archaic in thought and language? Virgil? Milton? Gray? What reason for it? How was the Faery Queen received? Is it as much read as the Pilgrim's Progress? Why not? What are its defects? Its merits? What qualities make Spenser Milton's favorite English poet? "Our sage, serious Spenser, whom I dare be known to think a better teacher than Scotus or Aquinas."—*Milton, Liberty of unlicensed Printing.*

(Write an analysis: see model in Appendix A. Study derivation, 310–349, in addition to the subjects before referred to.)

What is the first clause? What kind of clause? 404. What is its verb? 245. Its subject? 352. What objective combination? 407. What attributive combinations with *knight?* 405. What combination is *in* the sign of? *And* connects what? Are two propositions abridged in this? If so, give them! What was the oldest form of *a?* 216. When is *a* used for *an?* 216. Difference in meaning between *an* and *one?* 215. What is the meaning of *gentle* here? Connection of thought between

Yclad in mighty arms and silver shield,
Wherein old dints of deep wounds did remain,

---

the two meanings of it? Between *gentle* and *genteel?*—and *gentile?* What root letters common to *gentle* and *generous?*—and *generate?* 319, 4. Connection of thought between these and *kin, kind* from the corresponding Anglo-Saxon root? Force of *-t-* in *gen-t-le?* 321. Force of *-le* (=*-ile*)? 324. Other words from the same Anglo-Saxon root? *Knight* and *knave* originally meant what? (See before, page 48.) Connection between *knight=young man* and *knight* here? What kind of verb is *was pricking?* 279. Analyze it; parse *pricking* alone! Force of *-ing?* 266. Connection of thought between the common meaning and this? Is the use here by special figure, or was it current? (Current in Chaucer.) Does its use here make a poetical form? 491. Is *pricking on the plain* an equivalent for *spurring over the plain?* Difference between *on* and *over?*—and *in?* Meaning of *that* : *the* : : *one* : *an?* *The plain* is what plain? Is it characteristic of Spenser that his scenes are in no definite place or time? Connection of thought between *plain* and *plane?*—and *plan?*—and *piano?* Meaning of *y-* in *yclad?* Unabr. Gram., 339. Is it ever used now? Meaning of *mighty?* Connection of *might* and *may?* Force of *-y* in *mighty?* 313. Connection of thought between *arm* and *arms?*—*arms* and *armor?* Is the *shield* part of the *arms?* Connection of thought between *shield* and *shelter?* What poetic form in *silver shield?* 491. Who is the knight? (St. George.) What virtue does he represent? (Holiness.) What are the mighty arms? Ephesians, vi., 11+. What is the shield? Ephesians, vi., 16. On what adventure is St. George "pricking?" (To slay a dragon which laid waste the kingdom of the Lady Una's father.) What is represented thereby? (The Lady Una typifies the Church of England.) What legendary propriety in representing holiness by St. George? In sending him to slay a dragon? Which of Spenser's friends is depicted in this knight? (Sir Philip Sydney.) Sydney's character and life?

Next clause? Kind—subordinate or co-ordinate? 409. Substantive, adjective, or adverbial? 411. What noun or nouns does it describe? Connective? 396, IV. Composition of *wherein?* Grammatical equivalent for it? 396, VIII. Verb? Subject? 352. Attributive combinations with *dints?* 406. Rule for syntax of *marks?* 362. What kind of combination is *marks+of field?* 406. Pronominal element in *wherein?* 308. Other words from same? Its natural significance? 241.

The cruel marks of many a bloody field;
Yet arms till that time did he never wield:

Connection of thought between *old* and *aldermen?* Between *dint* and *din?* Is the root onomatopoetic? 305. What kind of blow does it imitate the sound of? How does it differ from *ding?* 305, III. Meaning of *wounds* here? What rhetorical figure? 458. Analyze *did remain;* parse *did* alone; *remain* alone! Give grammatical equivalents for both to show that *remain* is an infinitive! What kind of form is it called? 280. Is it really emphatic here? Is this unemphatic form used now? Had it become antiquated in Spenser's time? Why do young poets use it now? Is *did* a contraction for *doed?* 273. (No: *di-* is a reduplication.) Connection of thought between *remain* and *mansion?* Force of *re-?* 326. Pronominal element of *the?* 308. Natural significance of it? 228. Connection of thought between *cruel* and *crude? Crude* and Latin *cruor* (=*gore*, blood)? Force of *-el* in *cruel?* Difference between *cruel* and *bloody?* Why are the *marks* called *cruel?* What rhetorical figure? 458. In what number is *many?* Was it used in this sense in the singular in Anglo-Saxon? (See before, page 54+.) With or without the article? What other languages have a similar idiom? When did the article begin to be inserted? What was Horne Tooke's opinion about the *a?* (See also *Trench—English, Past and Present*, p. 147.) Is it correct? How can we tell that the article in semi-Saxon is not a corruption of *of?* Could the oblique cases *annes*, *aenne*, etc., be so? How does *many a field* differ in meaning from *many fields?* Is it a neat way of distributing *many?* Why should poets like the sound? What is meant by *field* here? What rhetorical figure is it? 459. Connection of thought between *blood* and *blossom*, *bloom*, *blow*—is *blood* so named from its color, or as being that which causes *blooming?* Force of *-y* in *bloody?* 313. What is the allegorical sense of *dints?* 432.—of *bloody field?* Mention some of the fields referred to!

Next clause? Kind? 409, 410. With what is it co-ordinate? Connective? Verb? Subject? 352. Direct object? 360. What combination is *till* the sign of? 407. Does *arms* mean offensive or defensive, or both? Meaning of *-s* in *arms?* Pronominal element in *that?* 308. Other words of same element; personal pronouns; relative; adverbs of time, place, manner; conjunction? Meaning of *-t* in *that?* 229. Other words in which it occurs? Is *did wield* a true emphatic form? 280. Analyze it; parse *did* alone; *wield* alone! Pronominal element

His angry steed did chide his foaming bit,
As much disdaining to the curb to yield:

---

in *he?* 308. Other words of same? Meaning? (Weak demonstrative.) Connection between *never* and *ever?* Rule for collocation of *he?* 356, 494.—of *arms?* 361, 494. Meaning of *wield?* Is it proper to speak of *wielding* a horse? What is the allegorical meaning of this clause? What propriety in it?

Next clause? Kind? 404. Verb? Subject? 352. Direct object? 360. Attributive combinations with *steed?* 406.—*bit?* *As—yield* is abridged for what clause? What part of speech is *as?* Is it often followed by an abridged sentence? Often a sign of apposition? Is this one of the cases in which some grammarians call it a pronoun? What syntax for it as such? What kind of combination is *much+disdaining?* 407.—*steed+disdaining?* *To* is a sign of what combination with *curb?* Any peculiarity of collocation in this clause? Pronominal element in *his?* 308. Meaning of it? Other words from it? Force of *-s* in *his?* Force of *-y* in *angry?* 313. Connection of thought between *anger* and *anguish?* Analyze *did chide;* parse *did* alone; *chide* alone! Is it a true emphatic form? Had this form become archaic in the time of Spenser? (Yes, in conversation and prose.) Is Spenser fond of it?—and of other archaisms? Are poets apt to be? Why? Meaning of *chide;* does it imply noise? Its past tense in the Bible? Genesis, xxxi., 36; Numb., xx., 3. Meaning of *foaming* here? Is it literally applied? Force of *-ing?* 266. Connection between *bit* and *bite?* Other meanings of *bit?* The connection of thought between them? Force of *-ing* in *disdaining?* Connection of thought between *disdain* and *deign?*—and *dignity?* Force of *dis-?* 326, 327, VIII. How different from *in-* in *indignant, indignity?* Pronominal letters in *the?* Their natural significance? 308. Is this use of *the* mentioned in 370? Connection of thought between *curb* and *curve?* Would you expect *curb* to come from the Norman French? Why? 43. *Steed* also? Why not? Difference between *steed* and *horse?* Is *steed* in the Bible? Is it any thing more than a sensation synonym for *horse?* Which would you expect Shakespeare to use more, *steed* or *horse?* (*Horse*, five times as often.) Milton? (*Steed.*) Why? Which is more expressive in sound? Is *steed* in Anglo-Saxon a poetic word? (No, its use is in connection with the raising of horses.) Connection of thought between *to* and *too?*—*yield* and *guilt?* (Anglo-Saxon *gyldan*, to pay.)

Full jolly knight he seemed, and fair did sit,
As one for knightly jousts and fierce encounters
fit.

Next clause? Kind? 404. Verb? Subject? What kind of combination is *he+knight?* 405.—*full+jolly?*—*jolly+knight?* Rule for collocation? 356. Is the peculiarity here mentioned in 494? Grammatical equivalent for *full?* 412. Is it obsolete in this use? What phrases with it survive? Is it in the Bible? Shakespeare? (Yes.) Milton? (Of course.) Connection of thought between *full* and *fill?* Common meaning of *jolly?* Connection of thought between *jolly* and *yule?* Force of *-ly?* 313. Connection between the common meaning and the meaning here? From what language is the meaning here taken? What trait of French character is suggested by the change in meaning from English *jolly* to French *jolie*, pretty, genteel? Has the meaning here ever been current in English? (*Jolly* and *full jolly* are common in Chaucer as descriptive of seemly vigorous young life, but perhaps are never applied to any one who is "too solemn sad." Milton imitates Spenser.) Connection of thought between *knight* and *knave?* Primary meaning of each? Pronominal element of *he?* Its force? Force of *-ed* in *seemed?* What verb is it equivalent to? Is it thought to be historically derived from the ancient form of *did?* (Yes.)

Next clause? Kind? 409, 410. Verb? Subject? What kind of combination is *fair+did sit?* 407. How was the adverb formed from an adjective in Anglo-Saxon? 293. How do we come to have so many adverbs of the same form as adjectives? 293. How is the poetic use of adjectives for adverbs explained? 293. Would you expect it to be common in Spenser? Why? Is this meaning of *fair* given in Worcester? Connection of thought between *fair* when used with *complexion* and when used with *dealing?*—and when used with *sit?* What part of speech is *as?* What complete proposition can be filled out after it? Is it often used as a sign of apposition? Difference in its meaning when used in apposition and in comparison? What kind of combination is *he+as one?* 406. Of what combination is *for* the sign? Give grammatical equivalents for the line, so that *and* may connect two propositions! Connection of *an* and *one?* 216. Force of *-ly* in *knightly?* 313. Connection of thought between *joust* and *jostle?* 313, 1.—and *adjust?* Force of *ad-?* 326. Connection of *fierce* and *ferocious?* What rhetorical fig-

II.

And on his breast a bloody cross he bore,
The dear remembrance of his dying Lord,

---

ure in *fierce encounters?* Connection of *encounter* and *counteract?*—and *contradict?* 327. Force of *en-?* 327. Connection of *fit* and *refit?*—and *counter-feit?* What peculiarity of collocation in the line?

Can an allegorical sense be seen in all the details of this description;—the steed; the chiding; the bit? Why depict Holiness as a jolly knight, etc.?

Next clause? Kind? 404. Verb? Subject? Direct object? 360. What combination is *on* the sign of? *Remembrance* combines with what? Kind of combination? 406. Attributive combinations with *remembrance?* 406. Translate the first line into literal prose, using no word beginning with *b!* Pronominal letter in *his?* Other words of same letter? Force of it? Force of *-s?* When is *a* used for *an?* 216. Relation of *an* to *one?* 217. Meaning of *-y* in *bloody?* 313. Connection of thought between *blood* and *bloom?* Between *cross* and *crusade?*—and *excruciating?*—and *curse?* Is *bloody* a better word here than *ruddy*, or *ruby*, or *scarlet*, or *blood-red?* Why? Would it not be well to interchange *bore* and *wore?* Why not? Pronominal element in *the?* Other words of same element? 308. Connection between *dear* and *darling?* 313, 343. Why should a diminutive form be used to express endearment? What letters common to *remembrance* and *memory?* Is the *-b-* euphonic or emphatic? Give other examples of *b* inserted after an accented *m* followed by *l* or *r!* (See before, page 58.) Meaning of *re-?* 326.—of *-ance?* 324. Is *remembrance* here used in its common sense? Would not *memento*, or *memorial*, or *souvenir* be better? Why not? Other examples of the use of *remembrance* in this sense? Isaiah, lvii., 8; Hamlet, iii. 1. Force of *-ing* in *dying?* 266. What part of speech is *dying* here? How do you tell whether an adjective or participle? Would *his Lord's death* be an exact equivalent for *his dying Lord?* What difference?

Next clause? Kind? 411. What noun does it describe? Verb? Subject? Direct object? What combination is *for* the sign of? Attributive combinations with *sake?* 406. Pronominal letters in *whose?* 308. Other words of same element? Is *who* a relative in Anglo-Saxon? 237. Explain how an interrogative turns into a relative! Give illustrative sentences! Meaning of *-se* in *whose?* Other words in which

For whose sweet sake that glorious badge he
wore,
And dead as living ever him adored:
Upon his shield the like was also scored,

---

the genitive termination is spelt *-se?* To which of the senses does *sweet* primarily refer? Connection of thought between *sweet* and *-suade* in *persuade?*—and *suavity?* Meaning of *sake?* Is it ever used now except with *for?* Connection between its meaning here and its old meaning—*i. e., cause in court, suit at law?*—between *sake* and *seek?* Pronominal element of *that?* It is equivalent to what gesture? 228. What does *-ous* in *glorious* mean? 324. Painters mean what by a *glory?* Connection of thought between *glare* and *glory?* Why *glorious* badge? Connection of thought between *badge* and *patch?* (Wedgwood's Etym. Dict.) Is the badge here a patch? Connection of thought between *beacon* and *badge* (<*old-English* bag, bagge—*Prompt. Parv.;* bagy—*Berners* <*Anglo-Saxon* beácn, *a token, sign*, especially *the cross*—e. g., *in hoc signo vinces*=mid thŷs beácnê ofersvîdhest—*Elene*, 92. The cross of the Crusaders was by eminence the badge, *Candida signa crucis juvenum præstantia pingunt pectora—Polit. Songs, Temp. Hen. III.*, p. 24. *Dutch* baake; *Ger.* baake; *Swedish* båk; M. *Latin* bagia, *a token, beacon*)? Connection with *beckon?*—with *beck?* Is *wore* a weak or strong verb? Why so called? 276. Connection between the meaning here and in Job, xiv., 19.

Next clause? Predicative combination? 405. Direct object? 360. *As* is a sign of what combination? What kind of combination is *adored* +*as living?* 407. Why is *living* called a factitive object? 360. Supply an ellipsis so as to make a predicative combination after *as!* What does *ever* combine with? Should it have a point before or after it? 543. Connection between *dead* and *die?* Force of *-ing* in *living?* 266. Which case is *-m* in *him* the sign of? 229. Are the objectives of other pronouns old datives? Why should the datives thus survive rather than the accusatives? Which oblique case occurs oftenest? Why? Force of *-d* in *adored?* What root letters are common to *adore* and *oratory?* Connection of thought between the common meaning of *oratory* and the place called an *oratory* by the Roman Catholics? Meaning of *ad-* in *adore?* 326.

Next clause? Kind? 404. Verb? Subject? *Upon* is the sign of

For sovereign hope, which in his help he had:
Right faithful true he was in deed and word;

---

what combination? Rule for the use of *the* here? 370, V. Of what combination is *for* the sign? Composition of *upon?* Are both parts significant here? Do the English now use *upon* less than Americans? —than old English? Connection of thought between *shield* and *shelter?* Meaning of *that* : *the* : : *one* : *an?* What termination is equivalent to *like?* 313. Give examples of its use! Composition of *also?* 303. Can you parse the parts as separate words here? *So* means how? Analyze *was scored;* parse *was* alone; *scored* alone! Connection of thought between *score* and *sheer, shorn?*—between *score* here and *score* (=20), and *on that score?* Grammatical equivalent to explain the meaning of *for?* Why is the word which Spenser spells *soveraine,* Milton *sovran* (<Fr. *souveraine;* It. *sovrano* <M. Lat. *superan*-us), spelt *sovereign?* Is it imagined to have some connection with the verb *reign?* What similar examples of illusive etymology? 342. Is it right to follow such a blunder? On what principle? Meaning of *sovereign hope?*

Next clause? Kind? 409, 411. What noun does it describe? Verb? Subject? Direct object? What combination is *in* the sign of? Does it complete or extend the predicate? 408. Pronominal letters in *which?* 308. Force of *-ch?* (A fragment of Anglo-Saxon *-lic*> Engl. *-like.*) Whose help? Is the rule in 373, XI., observed in this clause? Is *had* weak or strong? 247, 276. It is contracted for what? 273. Meaning of *-d?* Is it supposed to grow out of the old form of *did?* (Yes.)

Next clause? Kind? 404. Predicative combination? 405. What is *was* called? 353. *Faithful* combines with what? (Compare *solemn sad.*) *Right* combines with what? Kind of combination? 407. Give other instances of this use of *right!* Ps. xlvi., 5; cxxxix., 14; J. Cæsar, i., 3, etc. What titles contain it? Connection of thought between this meaning and the common one? Composition of *faithful?* 313. Connection of thought between *faith* (<old French *feid* <Lat. *fid-es*) and *fidelity?* Between *true* and *trust?* What obsolete word in Luke, xvii., 9, of the same root as *true?* Connection of thought between them? Pronominal element in *he?* 308. Adverbs of same element? Connection of thought between *he* and *hence?* Significancy of the element? (A weak demonstrative.) How does the plural (*they,* etc.) illustrate the sense of the singular—what is it the plural of in Anglo-Saxon? 229. What verb akin to *deed?* What does *and* connect? Supply the ellip-

But of his cheer did seem too solemn sad:

---

sis so as to give a predicative combination after *and?* Connection of thought between the meaning of *word* here and that in John, i., 1?

Next clause? Kind? 409, 410. Connective? Predicative combination? Is *he+did seem sad* a simple predicative combination? 408. What represents the copula? 353. What kind of combination is *solemn+sad?* *Of* is the sign of what combination? Meaning of *cheer?* (French *chère* down to the 16th century meant *head*, (2) *face*, (3) *mien;* Wycliffe, 2 Corinthians, iii., 7, reads *the glorie of his chere;* Mids. N.'s Dream, iii., 2, *pale of cheere.*) Connection of thought between these meanings and that in Paradise Lost, vi., 496?—and victuals, entertainment?—and in "three cheers?" In what phrase is it used in the Bible? Matt., ix., 2, etc. Analyze *did seem;* parse *did* alone; *seem* alone! Connection of thought between *too* and *to?* Between *solemnity* and *anniversary?* What are the root letters common to both? (*Emn=ann*< Latin *ann*-us, year.) Force of *sol-?* (All, every.) Its connection of thought with *sole, solitary?* Relation of *solemn* (<Latin *sol-ennis*) and *biennial* (<Latin *bi-ennis*)? Connection of thought between Anglo-Saxon *saed* (*=satiated*) and semi-Saxon, English *sad* (*tired out, sorrowful*)? In Chaucer, Spenser, Shakespeare, *sad* sometimes means merely *serious, grave;* is that its sense here? In the earliest English, and down to Spenser, *sad* occasionally means *heavy:*

> —"his hand, more sad than lump of lead,
> Uplifting high."—*Spenser.*

Is it the same word as the other *sad?* Meaning of *sad colors?* The connection of all these meanings? Has the divergence perhaps been promoted by resemblance to *set, settled?* Connection between *sad*, and *satisfy*, and *sate?* Is not *solemn sad* pleonastic? 473. (Shakespeare has *heavy sad, sad and solemn.*)

Next clause? Kind? 409. Predicative combination? 405. Objective combination? 407. Rule for collocation of *nothing?* 494. Analyze *did dread!* Composition of *nothing?* Is *did* from *doed?* 273. (See before, page 77.)

Next clause? Kind? 409. Verb? Subject? Objective combination? 407. Parse *ydrad!* What form like it has occurred before? Was it an archaism in the time of Spenser? (Yes.) Does it occur in Shakespeare? [It is ridiculed twice in Love's Labor Lost, i., 1; v., 2; occurs only once elsewhere (*yclad*), 2 K. Hen. VI., i., 1, if that is Shakes-

Yet nothing did he dread, but ever was ydrad.

What is this stanza called? 523. How many lines in it? What kind of foot is predominant? 483. How many feet in the first line? How many lines like it? What name is given to such lines besides iambic pentameter? 500. Why called *heroic?* How many feet in the ninth line? What other name for the iambic hexameter? 501. Why called an Alexandrine? 534. Which line rhymes with the first? With the second? With the sixth? Are there any other rhymes? Is any line unrhymed?

Scan the first line on page 75! Where is the cæsura? 483. Is any required by the sense? Is there any other foot than the iambus? Any approach to a spondee?—to a pyrrhic? In which foot? What alliteration? 491.

Scan the second line! All the feet pure iambics? Cæsura where?—required by the sense? What is the general principle about the expression given by an early cæsura? (See before, page 20.) If the cæsuras of the two first lines were to change places, would not the expression suit the sense better? How so? What alliteration in this line? Is there vowel alliteration? Is the repetition of *m* in *mighty* and *arms* alliteration? 491.

Scan the third line! Is *wherein* a pure iambus? What is it? Is *old dints* a pure iambus? Which syllable has more than the normal stress? What do you call the foot? 483. (See before, page 17.) Is *of deep* a pure iambus? *Wounds did* a trochee? 483. Was not *did* accented in such phrases in Spenser's time? How can you tell? Is the cæsura after *dints* or *wounds?* Why; is there any syntactical reason? Any metrical reasons connected with a trochaic place? What alliteration with *wherein?*—with *old?*—with *dints?*—with *m* in *remain?* What does *remain* rhyme with? Is the rhyme perfect? 484. What things are essential to a perfect rhyme?

Scan the fourth line! All pure iambics? What is the fourth foot? 483. Cæsura where? What alliteration? Is the rhyme perfect? The first four lines make what kind of stanza? 530.

Scan the fifth line! What is the third foot? Is *did* emphatic? Cæsura where? What alliteration? Is the rhyme perfect? It brings this line in unity with what others?

Scan the sixth line! Cæsura where? The seventh line! Cæsura after *disdaining?* What kind of foot is *-ing to?* Any repetition of similar sounds? Is the rhyme perfect? The eighth line! Cæsura where? Feet all pure? What alliterations? Is

---

peare.] In Milton? (Yes, in early poems.) Does Spenser invent the form *drad* for the rhyme? (Perhaps; but it is in Layamon.) Is it a weak or strong form? 247. Have many verbs once strong become weak? 276. Do weak verbs ever become strong? Give an instance! Why should Holiness be represented as bearing the cross on breast and shield? What custom is referred to? Why as *too solemn sad?* *Too solemn* for what? What special fitness in the last line? Why depict Holiness as dreading nothing?—being ever dreaded? [Continue similar questions through the extracts. Let the student write out questions covering all the subjects heretofore discussed.]

(Reprint from Prof. Child's Edition.)

III.

Upon a great adventure he was bond,
That greatest Gloriana to him gave,
That greatest glorious queene of Faery lond,
To winne him worshippe, and her grace to have,
Which of all earthly thinges he most did crave:
And ever, as he rode, his hart did earne
To prove his puissance in battell brave
Upon his foe, and his new force to learne;
Upon his foe, a Dragon horrible and stearne.

---

the rhyme perfect? The second four lines would make a stanza of what kind? 530. Why called elegiac? How are the two elegiacs united?

Scan the ninth line? How many feet in it? Cæsura where? What alliteration? What coupling with the eighth line besides the rhyme?—through *fair*, *fierce*, *fit*?—*jolly knight* and *knightly jousts*? [Go on with similar questions through the other stanzas.]

Synoptical.—Does this stanza admit every kind of musical delight belonging to blank verse? (See before, p. 17.) Is the rhyme a source of additional delight? 484, 493. Did the ancients ever use it? Who used it first? When? Is there any other stanza having as much variety in unity as this? What variety in the order of the rhymes?—in the frequency of their repetition?—in the length of the lines? What effect have the rhymes in bringing the whole to unity? What the Alexandrine? The stanza is called by Warton the *ottava rima* with a line added; have they any considerable resemblance in the order of rhymes or general expression? 532. What are the component parts of Spenser's stanza? 530, 501. Has it a true beginning, middle, and end? How many words must rhyme with the second line?—with the sixth? Is it easy to find so many rhyming words? What artifices does Spenser use to supply them? The introduction of unusual forms of verbs, etc.?—of obsolete words?—of foreign words?—of new words? Do the iteration of rhymes and fullness of stanza react on the thought? What kind of description do they promote? What faults?

("Those that write in rhyme still make
The one verse for the other's sake."—*Butler*.)

IV.

A lovely Ladie rode him faire beside,
Upon a lowly asse more white then snow;
Yet she much whiter, but the same did hide
Under a vele, that wimpled was full low;
And over all a blacke stole shee did throw:
As one that inly mournd, so was she sad,
And heavie sate upon her palfrey slow;
Seemed in heart some hidden care she had;
And by her in a line a milke-white lamb she lad.

What beauties? Is this stanza capable of epic prolongation and sustainment? Why not? In whose hands has it made the nearest approach to it? Has it been generally admired and often used? What did Lord Byron write in it? Is it specially suited to the Faery Queen and to Spenser? Explain how! Does Spenser rely as much as Milton for musical delight on variety of feet and of cæsuras? How many feet not pure iambics in the first stanza?—in the first nine lines of Paradise Lost? How many of the cæsuras in the same passage in Spenser are any thing more than a musical cadence? How many in Paradise Lost are vigorous syntactical pauses? Is there a similar uniformity in the ending of the lines in Spenser? A similar variety in Milton? Has Byron given the stanza more vigor in these respects? What poetical ornament does Spenser make most use of? 491. Whence is the power of alliteration to double the impressiveness of an image? Is it connected with the fact that each letter has its natural significance? Is that a reason why descriptives beginning with the same letter are so readily associated? Why so? What other reason? Which is oldest in the Northern languages, meter marked by alliteration, or by simple accent, or by quantity? 479, 491. Which way of marking meter springs most naturally from spoken language? From music? Why so? What other poetical ornament in the two last lines of the third stanza? (See before, pages 15, 32.) Is it used elsewhere in the same stanza? Is there any euphuism in this extract? (See before, page 73.) Does Spenser often use it? What epithets most fitly describe the music of Spenser's verse?—of Milton's?—of Shakespeare's?

Syntax.—Is there any line in the two stanzas just analyzed, at the end of which the sense is not complete? The first line is a clause of what

V.

So pure and innocent, as that same lambe,
She was in life and every vertuous lore;
And by descent from royall lynage came
Of ancient kinges and queenes, that had of yore
Their scepters stretcht from east to westerne shore,
And all the world in their subiection held;
Till that infernall feend with foule uprore
Forwasted all their land, and them expeld;
Whom to avenge, she had this Knight from far compeld.

---

kind? The second an attribute of what word? The third an attribute of what word? The fourth an attribute of what? Could syntax be more perspicuous? Any involution, transposition, condensation—any thing to obscure the flow of a most lucid, fluent, thoroughly trained mind? How does it compare with the opening of Paradise Lost?—of the Pilgrim's Progress? Is the rest similar in the ordering of clauses?

Diction.—Are the descriptive adjectives notably many or few? How many compared with Bunyan? (See before, page 14.) With Milton? (See before, page 34.) Is there any thing remarkable in the use of other parts of speech? How many words in the extract are not Anglo-Saxon? (Gentle, plain, arms, remain, cruel, disdaining, curb, jolly, joust, fierce, encounters, fit, cross, remembrance, glorious, adored, sovereign, faithful, cheer, solemn.) Is any reason given in 43 for the adoption of *gentle* in English? Give reasons for each Norman word! Is the average greater or less than usual? (See Appendix B.) Why should Spenser use less Anglo-Saxon than Shakespeare? Is there any reason growing out of the place where he lived?—the time when he wrote?—the rank of his family?—his education, profession, habits of study?—his associates?—his favorite authors?—(his prime favorite was "Dan Chaucer, well of English undefiled," F. Q., 4, 2, 32.)—the class for whom he wrote?—his themes?—his character? (See before, page 35+.) Why should he use more Anglo-Saxon than Milton? Has Spenser had any considerable influence on the English language? Have his peculiar forms come into common use? Has he been much studied by later poets, and imitated? To what extent by Milton? Thomson? Byron? Wordsworth? Keats? Lowell? Write an essay on the language and versification of Spenser covering the ground of the foregoing questions!

CHAUCER.

THE CANTERBURY TALES,

THE PROLOGUE.

INTRODUCTORY.—Write an account of the life and works of Chaucer; especially of the Canterbury Tales, his preparation for the work, the circumstances in which it was written, its character, influence, and fame.—(See Wright's Canterbury Tales, Tyrwhitt's Chaucer, Marsh's English Language and its early Literature, Child's Observations on the language of Chaucer.)

With what princes was Chaucer contemporary? With what great events? Did he take part in any campaign? Was he employed in state affairs? What was then the condition of the system of chivalry? Are any of the exploits of English heroes described in his works? Why not? What authors were his contemporaries in England?—in France?—Italy? Were any of them his acquaintances and friends? Did he visit foreign countries? What? When? Was there any thing like Protestantism in his time? Did he sympathize with the Reformers? What is known of his childhood and youth? Did he study at either University? How did he begin his literary career? From what language were his early writings translations? Is translating good training for original composition? How so? Was it more valuable in Chaucer's time than it is now? Why? To what extent were French and Latin used then in England? 42. Did he write much? At what age did he write the Prologue to the Canterbury Tales? What is the plan of the work? Is it carried out? Were all the Tales as now printed written after the prologue? Is Chaucer's fame greatest for the same merits as Shakespeare's—character painting?—other dramatic power?—love of nature?—humor?—pathos?—ease and geniality?—creative power in language? Are all of these shown in the Prologue? Which most? Is the general plan new? Is either of the Tales new? In what is the originality of Chaucer shown?

When was printing first used in England? How were books published in Chaucer's time? How copied? Was it usual for one to read aloud, and many others to listen and write down from the ear? Were manuscripts made in this way alike in spelling, punctuation, grammatical forms? Is a manuscript often found uniform in these respects?—or free from plain blunders? Why not? Was there any standard of English? Were the scriveners usually learned? Does Chaucer complain of them? (He says "unto his own scrivener:"

"Adam Scrivener, if ever it thee befalle,
Boece or Troilus for to write newe,
Under thy long locks thou maist have the scalle,
But after my making thou write more trewe!
So oft aday I mot thy werke renewe,
It to correct, and eke to rubbe and scrape;
And all is thorow thy negligence and rape."

Again:

"And for there is so gret diversité
In Englissh and in writynge of our tonge,
So preye I God that non myswrite the,
Ne the mysmetere for defaute of tonge.")

Did copyists alter what they wrote to the form of language of the time at which they wrote?—to the dialect of their own county? Have we any manuscripts of Chaucer written during his life? (The one printed by Wright, and followed in the extract here examined, is believed to be of that age.) Can we correct poetry better than prose? Why? Was Chaucer's poetry admired by his contemporaries for its harmony and regularity? What is his rank among English poets?

(Write an analysis: see model in Appendix A. Study Historical Elements, 1–66, Phonetic Elements, and Orthographical Forms, 67–171, and Appendix C, in addition to the subjects before referred to. Special attention is also drawn to synonyms.)

What is the first clause? What kind of clause? 409, 411. What kind of adverb? 411, III., 2. What verb does it modify? Connective? 396, IV. Verb? Subject? What are the phonetic elements of *whan* and *when*? 76, 121. The orthographic? 126, 127, 173. Were the letters written in the same order in Anglo-Saxon? 296. In which order are they now pronounced? 132. When did the present misspelling come into use? Where? Why? Which is right, *hwen* or *when*? Why?

Whan that Aprille with his schowres swoote

In what meter is this Prologue written? 500. Why called iambic? 483.—pentameter?—heroic? Is it rhymed? Which is most frequent, the single or double rhyme? 486. Had this meter been used before? Long ago by French poets; lately by Dante, Petrarch, Boccaccio: of what nation are these last? What had been the meters oftenest used by English poets? 501, 502, 490. Did this at once take its place as heroic? (No; it was long called "ryding rime," "most apt to write a merie tale."—*Guest, English Rhythms*, ii., 238.) Is the cæsura marked in the manuscripts? (Yes.) Were the words all pronounced in Chaucer's time as they are now? Can we tell usually how the words he uses were accented? How? Can we tell how many syllables each has? How? How many syllables are there in a typical line with a single rhyme?—with a double?

Scan the first line! Cæsura where? How many syllables in *Aprille?* Which is accented? How many in *showres?*—in *swoote?* Is the -*es* of plurals usually a syllable in Chaucer? (Yes.) Is *swoote* (= *swete*, 5967, etc. <Anglo-Saxon *svête*) regularly two syllables in Chaucer? (Yes; adjectives which end in *e* in Anglo-Saxon preserve the -*e* in Chaucer.) Is *Aprille* pronounced elsewhere as here? (Perhaps not. *Averi'l*, 6128; *A'pril*, 4426.) Does the accent of other words from the French vary? (Yes.) Why? Does *whan that* occur elsewhere? (Often; frequently one foot as here; many times *whan* is the last syllable of an iambus, 18.) What other reading of this line?

(Whanne that Aperyll wit his shoures swoote.
MS. Harl., 7333.

Whan that April. wit his shoures swote.
MS. Harl., 1758.)

Scan the former! The latter! Which is the most harmonious of the three? What objection to it—is *whanne* ever found dissyllabic? (Yes, 11718, 14695; but rarely.) Is *whanne that* elsewhere? (Possibly, 713.) What objection to the last reading? Are all the feet in our text pure iambics? How does the first vary? The third?

168–170. Which letters are the pronominal element? 308. Other English words of same element—pronouns, adverbs? 237–241, 291–296. Its natural significance? 241. Unabr. Gram., 167, IX. Give Grimm's law for change of English to Latin and Greek! App. C. Is *q* in Latin *quum* the right letter for *h* in Anglo-Saxon *hvaenne?* Of which case is -*n* the termination in Anglo-Saxon? 236. (Accusative.) Is Latin -*m* an accusative termination? Explain *who* : *when* : : Anglo-Saxon *hva* : *hvaenne* : : Lat. *qui* : *quum!* Give a grammatical equivalent for *when* to show its relation to *who, what!* (*At what time.*)

Next clause? Kind? 409, 411. In what syntax as a substantive? 411, I., 4. Do we still use this idiom? Connective? 237. Verb? Subject? Direct object? What combination is *with* the sign of? Kind of combination? 407. Attributive combinations with *schowres?*—with *drought?* What combination is *to* the sign of? What peculiarities of collocation in the clause? 494. What language is *that* from? 236. Its phonetic elements? 76. Orthographic elements? 173, 126, 127+. Is *th* surd or sonant? 149. What defect has the English alphabet in regard to these sounds? 154. Has the Anglo-Saxon the same defect? 163. How came the English to have it? Would it not be better to write *dhat* instead of *that?* (*t* : *th* : : *d* : *dh*.) Pronominal letters in *that?* 308. Other words of the same letters—article, pronouns, adverbs, conjunction? 217, 227, 229, 235, 236, 291, 296, 303. Natural significance of *th-?* 236. Unabr. Gram., 167. Give Grimm's law, and apply it to *th!* Is *t* in the Greek *to* (=the) the right letter? Meaning of *-t?* 229. What uses has *that?* 237. Connection of thought between its use as a demonstrative and as a relative?—and as a conjunction? Give examples to illustrate the connection! (Webster's Dict.) Phonetic elements of *Aprille?* 76. Explain the change of accent from Latin *Aprilis* to English *April!* 119, 10; 120, 1. Why should the English throw the accent back to the beginning of words more than the Romans or French? Any reason from the character of the Anglo-Saxon as compared with the Romanic tongues? Any from the character of the English people? Had the Anglo-Saxons a word for April? 348. (Easter-monadh.) Which is most expressive, the Anglo-Saxon or the Latin word? 348. Which best suited to poetic personification? Why does Chaucer use the Latin here?

What language is *with* from? 66. Phonetic elements? 76. Does the *th* represent the Anglo-Saxon *th* or *dh?* What defect in orthographic elements is suggested? 154. Connection of thought between *with* here and in *with*-stand, *with*-hold? Difference in use between *with* and *by?* From what language is *his?* 229. Phonetic elements? 76. Orthographic? 173. What orthographic defect? 124, 2: 154+. Pronominal letter? 308. Other words of same? 229, 291, 296. Meaning of *-s?* 192. Is *his* here masculine or neuter? Why do you think so? 229. Why not feminine? 181+. How is *schowres* now spelt? Phonetic elements? 76. What Anglo-Saxon does the *-es* represent? 195. (*-as*.) Does Chaucer regularly make it a full syllable? (See lines 7, 9, 11, 12, etc.) Difference between *shower* and *storm?* Present form of *swoote?* Phonetic elements? 76. Give the different meanings of *sweet!* Is the radical meaning a generic conception under which all the different uses are subsumed? What is it, then? What words akin through the Lat. *suavis?* Connection of thought with *suasion*, *assuage*, per-*suade?* Difference between *suavity* and *sweetness?* Natural significance of *sw?* Unabr. Gram., 167. Why are April showers called sweet? Phonetic

The drought of Marche hath perced to the roote,

Scan the second line! Cæsura where? How many syllables in *Marche?* Can you tell by the meter? (Not certainly: unaccented *e* final is regularly elided before *hath.*) Is it found elsewhere *March?* (Yes; 6128, 7364, 10361.) What is elision? 495. Is the letter which is said to be elided wholly silent or lightly glided over? Which is more harmonious here, a light *-e* or none? How many syllables in *perced?*—in *roote?* v. 425, 13389. *Roote* rhymes with what? Does it afford a reason for the use of *swoote* instead of *swete?* Are all the feet pure iambics? Does *to* have emphasis?

---

elements of *the?* 76. Orthographic? 127+. Does the *th* represent the Anglo-Saxon *th* or *dh?* 163. Pronominal letters? 308. Other words of same? 308. Origin of the definite article? 217, 218. What is meant by *one* : *an* : : *that* : *the* : : Lat. *ille* : Fr. *le* : : Lat. *unus* : Fr. *un?* Why should articles be found only in the later stages of language? 218. Phonetic elements of *drought?* 76. Orthographic? 173. What defects of the English alphabet are suggested? 124. Other English words of the same root as *dry* (<Anglo-Saxon √ *drug* or √ *drig*)? What Anglo-Saxon letter does the English *ou* represent? (*u.*) Explain the presence of the silent *gh!* Which are root letters? Which termination? 313, 5, *b.* What is Grimm's law to change English letters to Latin or Greek? App. C. What kind of letter is *d*—labial, palatal, or lingual? 80. Why so called? Name the labials! Is *d* smooth, middle, or rough? Which part of the law applies to it? ("Middle to rough.") What is the rough lingual? Connection of thought between *dry* and *thermometer?* Other words from Gr. √ *ther?* Grimm's law to change English to German? App. C. What letter does it give for *d?* What for *g?* Has Ger. √ *trock* in *trocknen* the right letters for Anglo-Saxon √ *drug?* What Anglo-Saxon letter corresponds to the Lat. *t* in *torrid* (<Lat. √ *torr*)? What German letter? Is *d* right in Ger. *dürr?*—*th* in the Engl. *thirst?* Is this the same root as that of *dry?* (No; only similar: to be compared, not confounded.) Phonetic elements of *of?* 76. Orthographic? 173. What defects of alphabet suggested? 124. From what language is *of?* 66, 332, 5. Root letter? Other prepositions or adverbs of same letter? 297, 299, 326, 327, 332. Connection of thought between *of* and *off?*—and *fro?*—*forth, fore?* Natural significance of *f?* Unabr. Gram., 167, XI. From what language is *Marche?* 348. Phonetic elements? 76. Orthographic? 173. Why does *r* modify the preceding vowel sound? 147. Alphabetic defects suggested by *ch?* 81, III., 124. From which sounds in Lat. *Martius* does the *ch* come? Explain the change! What was the Anglo-Saxon name of this month? 348. Any church

word from this Anglo-Saxon name? Which is more expressive, *Lenct-monadh* or *March?* Why has *March* superseded *Lenct-monadh?* 41–43. Other English words spelt *March?* Are they akin? Other accidental coincidences in English words—*e. g.*, What does *tender* mean? 341. Analyze *hath perced;* parse *hath* alone; *perced* alone! The direct object of *hath* alone? Was the perfect tense usually expressed in Latin and Greek by a perfect participle and auxiliary? (No. Unabr. Gram., 329.) Was it ever so expressed? (See Lat. Dict. *habeo;* Gr. Dict. ἔχω.) Give a history of the growth and establishment of this mode of expression in the modern languages? (Grimm, D. G., iv., 153+; Diez, Gram. Rom. Spr., ii., 109+.) What is the connection of thought between the meaning of the words separately and their meaning as a perfect tense, when the participle is transitive?—when it is intransitive? Is this use of intransitive perfects logical? (Latham, Engl. Lang., ii., 399+.) How is *hath* formed from *have?* 273. By what figure? 110. Its root? Termination? 273, 251, 5. From what language is *perce?* (Fr. *percer* <M. Lat. *pertusare* <Lat. *pertundere, pp. pertus-us.*) Phonetic elements? 76. Orthographic? 127+. How spelt now? Explain the change! Has the old pronunciation disappeared? What proper names akin? Is the imperfect *-ed* in *perced* a full syllable in Chaucer? When pronounced in one syllable what change of sound in *-d?* 86, 87. Is this change euphonic or necessary? Why? 85. Connection of thought between *per-* and *pierce?* 326, 17. Distinction between *pierce* and *bore?*—and *perforate?*—and *penetrate?*—and *prick?* Phonetic elements of *to?* 76. Root letter? Is it pronominal? 308. Its natural significance? Unabr. Gram., 167. Grimm's law to change English to Latin? App. C. What kind of letter is *t*—labial, palatal, or lingual? Why so called? Name the linguals? Is *t* smooth, middle, or rough? Which part of the law applies to it? ("Smooth to middle.") What is the middle lingual? Is *d* (in Lat. *ad*, to) the right letter? Which note in 370 describes the use of *the* here? Phonetic elements of *roote?* 76. When did the *-e* become silent? 46, 47. Is *boot* a perfect rhyme to *root?* 484+. Repeat the questions just now asked about Grimm's law and its application to *t* in *root;* what Latin letter corresponds to English *t?* Is the *d* right in Lat. *rad*-ix? What English words akin to *root* through Lat. *radix?* Connections between *root* and *liquorice?* Give grammatical equivalents for *drought* and *to the root!* 412. Is the drought to be thought of as having a root? What rhetorical forms here? 429+.

Next clause? Kind of clause? 409, 410. Co-ordinate with what clause? Connective? Verb? Subject? Direct object? What com-

And bathud every veyne in swich licour,

Scan the third line! Cæsura where? Is -*ud* a syllable? The third foot has how many syllables? What is it called? 483. Are the two last syllables of *every* used as a half foot by Shakespeare? (See before, page 66)—by more modern poets? Give quotations containing it! How many syllables in *veyne*? Can you tell certainly from this line? Is it elsewhere two syllables? Is -*e* elided here? Why? Which syllable in *licour* has the accent? It rhymes with what?

---

bination is *in* the sign of? Does *in licour* complete or extend the predicate? 408. Is it an adjunct of time, place, mode, or cause? 408. From what language is *and*? 44, 303. Is *d* the right letter for the Latin *t* (in *et*, *and*) in English or in German? (Grimm's law.) What is the German? (Und.) In exhibiting the kinship of *and* with Latin *et* (Gr. ἔτι, Sansc. *ati*), what is said of the *n*? Is its insertion frequent? (Yes; 321. Grimm, D. G., 3, 272.) Does it prevent the regular variation of the *d*? (Yes; Grimm, D. G., 3, 272.) Is the Latin *et* used in English? What does *etc.* stand for? Phonetic elements of *bathud*? What Anglo-Saxon is -*ud* from? (-*ôd*.) Explain the change from Anglo-Saxon *baedhôd* to *bathud!*—to *bath-ed!*—to *bathed!* Is the monosyllabic character of the English derived from the Anglo-Saxon? 95. Whence is it then? Is the orthographic change to *th* a defect? 163. Old form of *every*? 242. Its composition? 242. Distinction between *every* and *each*?—and *all*? Phonetic elements of *veyne*? 76. Orthographic elements? 127+. From what language is it? (<Fr. *veine* <Lat. *vena*.) Is the French *ei* regular for Latin *e*? (Yes; Diez, R. G., 1, 419.) Fr. -*e* <Lat. -*a*? (Yes; Diez, R. G., 1, 179.) Difference between *vein* and *artery*? Why should *vein* displace the Anglo-Saxon *vuht* and *aedre*, and *lancet* displace Anglo-Saxon *aedre-seax*? 43, 37, 38. Are the doctors still fond of new words from Latin and Greek? Phonetic elements of *in*? 76. What alphabetic defects suggested by it? 124, 81, 4. How is the long sound corresponding to *i* in *in* usually written? In how many ways can it be written? 153, 5. Give words corresponding to *in* in other languages! 326, 327, 332. Difference between *in* and *into*?—and *within*? Phonetic elements in *swich*? 76. Explain the change to *such!* Derivation? 242. Composition of Anglo-Saxon *swilc*, Goth. *svaleiks*? (Anglo-Saxon *sva*, so + *lic*, like.) Analogous forms in other languages? (Gr. τη-λίκ-ος, Lat. *ta-lis*, etc. Grimm, D. G., 3, 48.) How many phonetic elements may *ch* represent? 135. What Anglo-Saxon letter does it take the place of? 163, 242. Is the tendency common to all speech to glide from *c* (=*k*) to *ch*, to *sh*, to *c* (=*s*)? 135. Give examples of it

Of which vertue engendred is the flour,

Scan the fourth line! Cæsura where? How is *vertue* accented? It retains the accent of what language?—like what words before? Can you tell from this line whether -*e* in *vertue* is a syllable? Why not? What is the fourth foot? Is *is* emphatic?

---

in words derived from Latin and Greek? Phonetic elements of *licour?* 76. Explain the change of accent in *liquor!* 98. Why has the spelling *liquor* come into use? Does it agree with the sound, or is it a revival of the Latin? Is Chaucer's -*ou*- a regular change for Fr. -*eu*- in *liqueur*, from Lat. -*o*- in *liquor?* (Diez, 1, 148.) Which letters in *liquor* are root? Which termination? Other words of the same root? Distinction between *liquor* and *fluid?*

Next clause? Kind? 411. It describes what noun? Verb? Subject? What combination is *of* the sign of? Does *of which vertue* complete or extend the predicate? 408. What kind of adjunct is it? 408. Give a grammatical equivalent for it! 412+.—for *engendred is!*—*in swich licour?* Distinction between *of* here and in line second? Connection of thought? Which is nearer the primary sense? (See above, page 92.) Phonetic elements of *which?* 76. Orthographic? Its pronominal letters? 308. What word in the first line is akin? What questions were asked about that? What is *which* from? (Anglo-Saxon *hvilc.*) What is the force of the -*ch* <Anglo-Saxon -*lc?* (<Anglo-Saxon -*lic*> Engl. -*like*, -*ly*.) Other words in English of same termination? 242. Analogous forms in other languages? (Ger. *welch*, Gr. πηλίκος, Lat. *qualis*. Grimm, D. G., 3, 48+.) What peculiarity in the use of *which* here? Does it mean *whose* or *which kind of?* Do the English vulgar still use *which* in anomalous ways? (See, *e. g.*, Dickens.) What is suggested about the origin of vulgarisms? (Before, page 52.) Phonetic elements of *vertue?* 76. Its derivation? 327, IV. English words allied through Lat. *vir*, a man? Connection of thought between *virtue* here and *vir?* What remarks on national character are suggested by the meanings of Lat. *virtus*, It. *virtu*, Engl. *virtue?* (16+. Trench, Study of Words.) Why should our word of this sense be Norman? 62, 63. Did it probably come through the natural philosophers or the priests? Is it in the Bible? (Mark, v., 30; Phil., iv., 8.) Phonetic elements of *engendred?* 76. What sound had *g* in Latin and Anglo-Saxon? Before what letters has the sound changed? 138. Has any other consonant changed before the same letters? 135. Why should these changes occur before *e* and *i* more than before *a* or *o?* What is the

5. Whan Zephirus eek with his swete breeth

Scan the fifth line! Cæsura where? Some of the manuscripts have it after *eek* (spelt *eke*); in that case, how many syllables in *eke*? How scan the line? Which is more harmonious here for the second foot, *-irus* or *-irus eek*? Might both occur in Milton or Shakespeare as well as Chaucer? What foot like the latter on page 24?—page 42? Is *eek* elsewhere one syllable? (Yes; v. 41, 96, and often.)—two syllables? (Not in the Prologue, but sometimes as a rhyme, 4479, 5136.) How many syllables in *swete*? (Before, v. 1.) What does *breeth* rhyme with? What kind of foot is the second?—the third?

---

change of *-dre* to *-der* called? 110, IX. Root letters of *engendred*? 319, 4. Prefix? 327, IX. Formative suffix? 324, 2. Termination? Whence the inserted *-d*? 110, V. Give other examples! (*Tender* <Lat. *tener; gender; cinder;* Gr. ἀνδρός, etc.) Make a rule for it! (Diez, R. G., 1, 206. Greek Gram.) Explain it from the position of the organs uttering *n* before *r*! Analyze *is engendred;* parse *is* alone; *engendred* alone! Is the passive of other languages formed in a similar way? What tenses in Latin are plainly so? What other way of denoting the passive in French? In Latin? Greek? How should a reflective pass into a passive sense? Which kind of verbs in 286 best illustrate the change? Phonetic elements of *is*? What alphabetical defect? 170, 124. Derivation? 274, III. Repeat questions upon *the* from page 92! Which note in 370 describes its use here? Phonetic elements of *flour*? 76. Are they the same as those of *flower*? Which has the better orthographic elements? Derivation? (<Fr. *fleur* <Lat. *flos*, gen. *flor*-is.) Is Engl. *ou* regular for Fr. *eu* and Lat. *o*? (Before, *licour*.) Connection of thought between *flower* and *flour*? How late is the separation of these two words? (Before, page 60.) Distinction between *flour* and *meal*? *Flower* and *blossom* and *bloom*?

Next clause? Kind? 411. It modifies what verb? It represents what kind of an adverb? Its verb? Subject? Direct object? What does *eek* combine with? What combination is *with* the sign of?—*in* the sign of? For what sentence is *and heeth* abridged? Attributive combinations with *breeth*?—*holte*?—*croppes*? What case would *breeth* take in Latin?—what *holte*?—*croppes*? Has *whan* occurred before? What questions undecided there does this line help to answer? From what language is *Zephirus*? Phonetic elements? 76. Are the Roman letters here those regularly used for the Greek letters in Ζέφυρος? What English from it? Connection of thought between the wind and the cloth so named? Would a wind from this direction have these proper-

Enspirud hath in every holte and heeth

Scan the sixth line! Cæsura where? Is *-ud* a syllable? Is *holte* two syllables? Any foot not a pure iambus? What is the fourth?

ties every where? Where does it? Why? How is *eek* spelt now? Which is better, *eek* or *eke?* 165. Why? Its derivation? (<Anglo-Saxon *eác*.) Difference in use now between *eke* and *also?* What other English word spelt *eke?* Connection of thought? Grimm's law to change English to Latin? What kind of letter is *k*—labial, lingual, or palatal? Name the palatals! Is *k* smooth, middle, or rough? Which part of the law applies to it? ("Smooth to middle.") What is the middle palatal? Is *g* in Lat. *augeo* (*augment*) the right letter? Has *with* occurred before? Repeat the questions! Has *his* occurred before? Repeat the questions! Has *swete* occurred before? Repeat the questions on *swoote!* What of the spelling in old books and manuscripts? What was the first standard of orthography recognized in England? When was Johnson's Dictionary printed? Derivation of *breeth?* (<Anglo-Saxon *brædh*, odor, reek.) Connection of thought with *broth?* Analyze *enspirud hath;* parse *enspirud* alone; *hath* alone! How much of *enspirud* is root? (<Lat. √*spir*, breathe.) Prefix? 326, 327. Which is used now, the Latin or Romanic form? What is the termination? Origin of *-ud?* (<Anglo-Saxon *-ód*.) Connection of thought between the primary meaning and the theological? Other words from same root? Connection of thought between √*spir* and *spirit?* Distinction between *inspire* and *inspirit?*—and *animate?* What questions upon *hath* were asked before?—upon *in?*—*every?* Does *in* mean the same as in verse third? Derivation of *holte?* (<Anglo-Sax. *holt*: Ger. *holz*.) Do words ending in a consonant ever assume the syllable *-e* in Chaucer? (Often.) How is it explained? Do the oblique cases have a syllable more than the nominative? (Yes.) Does the word used in modern languages often come from the oblique forms of the old word? (Yes.) Why? How many oblique cases are there? Is any one of them used as often as the nominative? Are all together used much oftener? Give examples from the Latin! Why *sermon* <Lat. *sermo?*—*patent* <Lat. *patens?* (So Ital. *radice* <Lat. *radix*, Ital. *libertate* <Lat. *libertas*, Romaic λαμπάδα <Gr. λαμπάς, etc.) Is *holte* here an oblique case? Is the orthography certain? (No: the manuscripts given by Guest both have *holt*.) Do you think *holt* or *holte* better? Why? Is *holt* still in use? Why should "*holt and heath*" live longer than *holt* alone? 491.

The tendre croppes, and the yonge sonne

Scan the seventh line! Cæsura where? How many syllables in *croppes?* Does plural *-es* usually make a syllable? What example before? How many syllables in *yonge?* "The definite form of monosyllabic adjectives ends in Chaucer in -e"—what is meant by the "definite form?" (When the adjective is preceded by the definite article, by any other demonstrative, or by a possessive pronoun.) What reason for this *-e?* (The Anglo-Saxon adjective has a special declension when definite, many forms of which end in *-an*> old English *-en*> *-e*.) What kind of foot is the third?

What effect has alliteration in giving currency to proverbs and other phrases? Give illustrations! Latin for *and?* Phonetic elements of *heeth?* Which orthography is better, *heeth* or *heath?* 165. What name for the *ee?* 165. Do *heath* and *breath* now rhyme? 484+. Are the vowel sounds of the Anglo-Saxons exactly known? (No.)—of the time of Chaucer? (No.) Was there much variety in the pronunciation of different places?—and persons? (Yes.) Is this a natural consequence of a mixture of races and languages? Why? What is believed to be the sound of the Anglo-Saxon *ae?* (Like *e* in *there*, fluctuating to *a* in *fate*.) What other words of the same root as *heath?* Its connection of thought with *heathen?* What other word illustrates the same connection? Difference of meaning between *heathen* and *pagan?*—and *gentile?* Which note in 370 describes the use of *the* here? Phonetic elements of *tendre?* 76. What figure is the change of *-dre* to *-der?* 110. Are the phonetic elements the same? (No.) Has the change of sound from Fr. *-re* to Engl. *-er* usually been denoted by change of spelling? Give other examples! Is this change made in all similar cases? How about *theater* <*théâtre*, *center* <*centre*, *meter?* What lexicographer gives *-er* in these words? Should he be followed? If not, why not? 166–170. How is this termination written in Anglo-Saxon? (Before, page 33.) In the old classic English? (Before, pages 87, 36, 33.) In German? (Theater.) In Latin? (*Hexameter.*) Is the *d* in *tendre* <Lat. *tener* emphatic or euphonic? Rule? (Before, verse 4.) Phonetic elements in *croppes?* 76. Is more than one *p* articulated? Why more than one printed? 165. What is the root?—termination? What Anglo-Saxon termination does *-es* represent? 105. Is it a syllable in Chaucer? (Verses 1, 9, 14, etc.) Is there any English word of the same meaning as *croppes?* Why should the Anglo-Saxons need such a word more than we?

Next clause? Kind? Co-ordinate copulative with what? Connective? Verb? Subject? Direct object? 360. Is *course* an object or

Hath in the Ram his halfe cours i-ronne,

Scan the eighth verse! Cæsura where? Is the first foot a pure iambus? Any other foot which is not? How many syllables in *halfe?* Is it of the definite declension? (Before, verse 7.) Why? What does *ironne* rhyme with? Is it a single or double rhyme? 486.

---

effect? What is meant by a cognate objective? *Ram* combines with what? Kind of combination? 407. Is it an adjunct of time, place, manner, or cause? 408. Grammatical equivalent for *yonge sonne?*—for *in the Ram?*—for *halfe cours?* Translate the whole clause into scientific statement! Is the same time described here as in the two first lines? What questions have been asked about *and?*—*the?* Phonetic elements in *yonge?* 76.—orthographic? What alphabetic defects are suggested by *young?* 154+. Root of *yonge?* Termination? What Anglo-Saxon does the *-e* represent? (The definite declension in Anglo-Saxon is different from that given in 209; the nominative singular masculine ends in *-a.*) What other languages have a peculiar definite declension for the adjective? What is the peculiarity of this declension? (The use of *n* in the endings of all the cases. In Anglo-Saxon it is rather an absence of declension; all distinctions are blunted into a nearly uniform *-an;* in Semi-Saxon [Layamon] this has further weakened to a uniform *-e*, though the adjective is pretty fully declined when alone.) Why should the endings fall away in this use first? Does the article itself show the case? Are the adjective and noun taken together like a compound noun? Phonetic elements of *sonne?* 76. Which is peculiar to the English? 131. Gender of *sun?* Why? 181, 182. Anglo-Saxon *sunne* is feminine, *mona* (moon) masculine—why? (Compare before, page 58.) Whence the change? What questions before upon *hath?* Root of *ironne?* Prefix? Origin of *i-?* (<Anglo-Saxon *ge-;* see Unabr. Gram., 339.) Has it occurred before in these extracts? Was it obsolete in the time of Spenser? Termination? (267; Anglo-Saxon *-en* > *-e.*) What questions on *in* before?—on *the?* Meaning of *Ram* here? Connection of thought between this and the primary meaning? Why is *Aries* used now instead? What adverb of the same pronominal letter as *his?* 308. Phonetic elements of *halfe?* 76. What orthographic defects? 124. Is the *l* of any use? Grimm's law to change English to German? (App. C.) What kind of letter is *f*—labial, lingual, or palatal? Name the labials! Is *f* smooth, middle, or rough? Which part of the law applies to it? What is the middle labial? Is *b*

And smale fowles maken melodie,

Scan the ninth verse! Cæsura where? How many syllables in *smale?* Why? (The plural of monosyllabic adjectives ends regularly in *-e*.) Was the ending the same in Anglo-Saxon? 209. Why should monosyllables hold their inflections longer than other words? How many syllables in *fowles?* What Anglo-Saxon termination does *-es* here represent? 195. How many syllables in *maken?*—in *melodie?* Is any foot not a pure iambus?

---

right in German *halb?* How much of *halfe* is root? Termination? Of what declension is *-e* the regular termination in monosyllables in Chaucer? (Before, page 98.) Phonetic elements of *cours?* 76. What orthographic defects suggested by *course?* 124, 135, 130, etc. Derivation of *cours?* (<Fr. *cours* <Lat. *curs*-us <*curr*-o, pp. *curs*-us, run.) Other English words of the same root? Is Fr. *ou* <Lat. *u* regular? (Yes; Diez, R. G., 1, 155.) Why is *-us* dropped? 195, 196. How are the relations expressed in modern languages which used to be expressed by case-endings? 298. Which are more precise, prepositions or case-endings? Is the natural progress of thought from indefinite notions to more precise perceptions and judgments? How was this natural progress aided in French and English by the mixture of nations? Is it easier to learn the radical part and meaning of words or the inflections? How does this fact affect language when strange nations mix? (Marsh, E. L., 367.) Is Engl. *course* from Fr. *cours* or Fr. *course* <M. Lat. *cursa?*

Next clause? Kind? Co-ordinate with what? 410. Connective? Verb? Subject? Direct object? Is *d* in *and* right for Latin *t* in *et* according to Grimm's law? (Before, page 94.) Phonetic elements of *smale?* Orthographic defects in our present spelling of it? 124. Why *ll?* 165. Root of *smale?* Termination? 209. Difference between *small* and *little?* Phonetic elements in *fowles?* 76. Orthographic defects in present spelling? 124. By what figures is *fowl* made from Anglo-Saxon *fugel?* 110. Difference now between *fowl* and *bird?* Does *fowl* mean *bird* in the Bible? Give examples! On what principle came *fowl* to be specially applied to the gallinaceous tribe? Illustrate from the use of *Bible* (=book), *deer* (=wild animal), *venison* (=hunting)! Explain how *bird* (<Anglo-Saxon *brid*, brood, young of birds) came to have its present general sense! Which diminutive force has *bird*, endearment or contempt? 343. Why should a word of endearment grow into more and more use for the winged race? (Compare *poultry*, *pigeon*, etc.; also look at Concordances of Shakespeare and the Bible to see

10. That slepen al the night with open yhe,

Scan the tenth line! Cæsura where? 483. How many syllables in *yhe?* It rhymes with what?

in what connections *bird* is used, and in what *fowl.*) Root of *maken?* Termination? 252. How late is plural *-en* found? 47. What other terminations of the present tense, plural number, in Chaucer? (*-eth* [-ith, -th] and *-e.*) What was the Anglo-Saxon form? (*-ath* in the indicative.) Whence the *-en?* (In Anglo-Saxon the subjunctive present has *-an* (*-en*), and the imperfect indicative has *-on*, subjunctive *-on*, *-en.*) Why should the *th* be driven out by these forms? Was it hard to pronounce? (The Normans could not sound it well.) What has displaced it in the singular? In what sense does Chaucer use *making* on page 89? What analogy in formation between *poet* and *maker*, the old word for it? Relation between *make* and *machine?* Phonetic elements of *melodie?* 76 What does it rhyme with? What traces of the *-ie* in modern English? 184, III. The stem of *melodie?* Termination? (*-e.*) Roots? Is *mellifluous* akin?—*melasses?* What words akin through √*oed?* 330. Difference between *melody* and *harmony?* Why should words of this sense not come from Anglo-Saxon? 43. What words connected with music and poetry are from the Anglo-Saxon? What inferences about the Anglo-Saxon and English musicians and poets?

Next clause? Kind? 409, 411. It describes what noun? Connective? 376. Verb? Subject? Does *night* complete or extend the predicate? 408. Is it an adjunct of time, place, mode, or cause? 408. What preposition would express the relation between it and *sleepen?* Which is better, to use a preposition, or not? Why? 360, VII. What the case and syntax of *night* in Latin?—in Greek? Is a preposition used in these languages? What kind of combination is *sleepen*+*yhe?* 407. What kind of adjunct is *yhe?* 408. How would it be expressed in Latin?—Greek?—German? What attributive combinations in this clause? 406. What questions have been asked about *that?* (Before, page 91.) Natural significance of *th?* 228. Explain the transition from a demonstrative to a relative! Phonetic elements of *sleepen?* 76. What orthographic expedient? 165. Root? Termination? Has this termination occurred before? Distinction between *sleep* and *slumber?*—and *doze?*—*drowse?*—*nap?*—*repose?* Phonetic elements of *al?* Explain *ll* in *all!* 165, 5. Distinction between *all* and *every?* Etymological connection between *all* and *lonely?* What questions upon *the* before? How

So priketh hem nature in here corages:—

Scan the eleventh line! Cæsura where? Why after *nature* rather than *hem*? How many syllables in *nature*? Which is accented? What figure? 405. When is a final vowel elided in Chaucer? How many syllables in *here*? Is it a monosyllable elsewhere? (Yes; 32, 1018, and every where.) Which syllable in *corages* is accented?

does *all the night* differ from *all night*? Phonetic elements of *night*? 76. Orthographic defects? 124. Why retain *g*? 165. Why *h*? 166. Grimm's law to change English to Latin? App. C. Does *h* represent a labial, lingual, or palatal? App. C. What are the palatals? Is *h* for the smooth, middle, or rough? Which part of the law applies to it? What is the smooth palatal? Is *c* in Latin *noct*-is right? What English from this Latin stem? Difference between *nightly* and *nocturnal*? What is suggested of the Anglo-Saxon mode of reckoning time by *fortnight, sennight*? Grimm connects *nigh* with *night*—*i. e.*, that which draws *nigh*, the impending, the swift-coming, θοὴ νύξ—*Homer;* to whom and when would such a conception of night be the natural one? What questions before on *with*? What number is *open*? Has the plural a case-ending -*e*, as in *smale*, verse 9? Why should monosyllables retain their terminations longer than other words? Stem of *open*? Root? What preposition of same root? Connection of thought between *up* and *open*? What other derivatives in -*en*? 285. Phonetic elements of *yhe*? 76. Stem? Case-ending? From what Anglo-Saxon case-ending? (-*e*). Plural in Chaucer? (*yhen;* 184, VI.). Grimm's law to change English to Latin? Which kind of letter does the *h* in the stem *yh* represent? Name the palatals! Which does *h* represent? Which part of the law applies to it? What is the smooth palatal? Is c in Latin *oc*-ulus the right letter? Give words akin to *eye* through the Latin! Relation between *ocular evidence* and *eye-witness*? Is *g* in German *auge* the right letter for Latin c, English *h*? (App. C.)

Next clause? Kind? 410, IV. What conjunction would express the connection? Verb? Subject? Direct object? What does *corages* combine with? In what case and syntax would it be in Latin?—in Greek? Grammatical equivalent for *in here corages*?—for *so priketh*? Translate the line into scientific statement! Pronominal letter in *so*? 308. Other words of same element? Connection of thought between *so* and *she*? Root of *priketh*? Personal ending? Whence *ck* in English *prick*? 141, 165, 6. Natural significance of -*th*? 308. Is it the proper pronominal element to represent the third person? What Latin letter should be used for it according to Grimm's law? (App. C.) Is *t*

Thanne longen folk to gon on pilgrimages,

Scan the twelfth line! Cæsura where? How many syllables in *thanne?* Is it always one syllable in this text? (Often; not always.) Do all the manuscripts read *thanne?* (No; MS. Harl., 1758.—Guest, E. R., 1, 215, reads *than.*) Does *than* ever occur in this text? (Yes.)

---

in Latin *amat* right? Difference between *prick* and *pierce?* Are they akin? What do we now use for *hem?* Its pronominal letter? 308. Which case is *-m* the ending of? 195, 209, 236. What is the dative plural of *he* in Anglo-Saxon? 229. What Anglo-Saxon is *them* from? 229, 236. Do the English personal pronouns borrow other forms from the Anglo-Saxon demonstratives? How is it in Latin and Greek,—do demonstratives pass into personals? Explain the tendency! Phonetic elements of *nature?* Accent where? Is it fixed in Chaucer? (No.) What words accented like *nature* before? What Latin letter does *-e* represent? (Before, page 94.) Root? Termination? 324, 5, 11. Gender? 182. From what is *here?* (<Anglo-Saxon *heora.*) 229. What English has displaced it? Phonetic elements of *corages?* Root? Suffix? 327. Plural sign? Other words of same root? Connection of thought between *cordial* and *courage?* Is the *-ou-* in *courage* right for Latin *-o-?* (Before, *licour, flour.*) Whence French plural *-s?* Is *-s* a more common plural sign in Latin or Anglo-Saxon? (Latin.) What about the accent of *corages* compared with *courage?*

Next clause? Kind? 404. What does *to gon* combine with? Kind of combination? 408. Grammatical equivalent for *to gon* containing a predicative combination? Phonetic elements in *thanne?* From which pronoun is it? 236, 291, 303. Pronominal letters? 308. Termination? From what case-ending is *-nne?* 236. Corresponding adverb from the interrogative? 308. Meaning of *when* and *then* as accusatives of *what* and *that?* 360, VII. (Before, page 90.) Phonetic elements of *longen?* 76. Do you hear the *o* sounded oftener like *o* in *not*, or *aw* in *law?* Which is right? Root of *longen?* Personal ending? Why plural? Rule? Other words of same root? 319. Connection of thought between the adjective *long* and this verb? Distinction between *long* and *incline?*—and *desire?* Phonetic elements in *folk?* 76. Why retain the *l?* Is *k* a labial, lingual, or palatal?—smooth, middle, or rough? Is *g* in Latin *vulg*-us the right letter for it? Grimm's law? (App. C.) What words akin through the Latin? Connection of thought between *folk* and *vulgate?* What is the present use of *folk, folks?* Why less used than formerly? What questions about *to* on page 93? Is its meaning here the

And palmers for to seeken straunge strondes,

Scan the thirteenth line! How many syllables in *straunge?* What rule? (Before, page 100.)

---

same as there? 388, II. What case is *to* the sign of in Latin, Anglo-Saxon, etc.? In languages with case-endings, does the infinitive take a dative form? 263, 389. (Bopp, § 884+.) Is it coupled in other languages with prepositions similar in meaning to *to?* (Bopp, § 880+.) Does *to* with the infinite always have its proper meaning as a preposition? 263. How comes it to be used with an infinitive in the nominative? Can you give examples of nouns or pronouns in which oblique cases have driven out the nominative? (Before, p. 40, 97.) What inference in regard to the frequency with which remote objects occur? Why should they so occur? Root of *gon?* Termination? What mode does *-n, -en* indicate in Chaucer? When did it cease to be used? 47. What other preposition of the same fundamental letter as *on?* Connection of thought between *in* and *on?* Through what classes of languages does this preposition run? 25+. Difference between *on* and *upon?* Give uses of *upon* which are called Americanisms? Is *upon* used in older English where *on* is now used in England? (Before, p. 15, 51.) What contraction of *on* is sometimes used? 290. What is the sign of the plural in *pilgrimages?* From what languages is the *-s* of this word? (Before, page 103.) Are all the statements in 64 accurate? Is *pilgrimage* a primary derivative? 320. What affix has it? 327. Meaning of *-age?* Derivation of *pilgrim?* Which are root letters? (*-gr-*). What Anglo-Saxon letters correspond by Grimm's law? (App. C.) Other words from Lat. *ager* : Anglo-Sax. *acer* > Engl. *acre?* What Latin prefix does *pil-* represent? 326, 17. What Latin suffix does *-im* represent? 324, 3, 12. Explain how these elements are put together in the Latin *peregrinus!* Explain the change into *pilgrim!* Difference between *pilgrim* and *palmer?*—between *pilgrimage* and *journey?*—*tour?*—*excursion?*

Next clause? Kind? Verb? Subject? What does *for* add to the sense? Is it always equivalent to *in order?* What similar preposition is used in French? (Pour.) When did *for to* cease to be used? Is it in the Bible?—in Shakespeare? (Before, page 41.) What combination is *for* the sign of?—*to?*—the second *to?* Attributive combinations with *halwes?* Meaning of *halwes?* Other English words from same root? Meaning of *ferne halwes?* (Distant saints.—*Wright.* Others

To ferne halwes, kouthe in sondry londes;
And specially, from every schires ende
Of Engelond, to Canturbury they wende,
The holy blisful martir for to seeke,
That hem hath holpen whan that they were seeke.

Scan the fourteenth line! How many syllables in *kouthe?* Rule? Why is *-e* elided?

The fifteenth line! How many syllables in *schires?*—in *ende?* Are both according to Chaucer's usage?

The sixteenth line! How many syllables in *Engelond?*—in *Canterbury?*—*wende?*

The seventeenth line! Are all the words pronounced as now? How many syllables in *seeke?*

The next line! All the words pronounced as now? (Before, page 104.) How many syllables in *seeke?* How many examples have we had of a plural adjective with the sign *-e?* (Go on with similar questions through the extracts.)

Synoptical.—How many feet are there in this extract not pure iambics? How many in the same number of lines at the beginning of Paradise Lost?—of the Faery Queen? Is there a sufficient variety of feet for musical delight? Does the cæsura play as prominent a part in Chaucer as in Milton?—or in Shakespeare? In how many different places is it found in this extract? Are the syntactical pauses well adjusted? They usually fall where? Does Chaucer usually make his full stops at the end of the second rhyming line? Are stops at the end of the former rhyming line more frequent than in Pope and his successors? What is the effect of them? Are there more single

---

have read *serve halwes.*) What English of the same root as *ferne?* Connection of thought between *kouthe* and *uncouth?* Why were *palmers* so called? Mention *halwes* in sundry lands which were most sought at this time? What record of these palmers in the word *saunter?*

Next clause? Kind? Verb? Subject? What does *specially* combine with? Attributive combinations with *ende?* Connection of thought between *specially* and *species?* Why should such a word be from the Latin? It is a technical term of what science? Connection of thought between *schires* and *shear?*—and *share?*—and *shore?* Composition of *Engelond?*—of *Canterbury?* Connection between *wend* and *went?*—*blisful* and *blessed?*—*holy* and *halwes?*—and *hale?*—and *whole?*—*heal?*—and Gr. *καλός* (*kalos*), beautiful? Has it right letters by Grimm's law? Connection of thought between *martyr* and Gr. *μάρτυρ*, a witness?—between *seek* and *sake?* The older form of the infinitive *seeke?* (verse 13.)

Next clause? Kind? What noun does it describe? Next clause? How many clauses in verse 18? What kind is the last? (Before, verse 1.) (Similar questions through the extracts.)

Byfel that, in that sesoun on a day,
In Southwerk at the Tabbard as I lay,
Redy to wenden on my pilgrimage
To Canturbury with ful devout corage,
At night was come into that hostelrie
Wel nyne and twenty in a companye,
Of sondry folk, by aventure i- falle
In felaschipe, and pilgryms were thei alle,
That toward Canturbury wolden ryde.
The chambres and the stables weren wyde,
And wel we weren esud atte beste.

---

or double rhymes in this extract? Is their succession well managed? Point out examples! Is the succession of vowels and consonants happily chosen? Is the rhythm happier in this respect than that of modern poets? What advantage do the terminations now obsolete give? Are they mostly vowels or other easy utterances? Give examples to show how they affect the flow of the verse! Does he use elision more than is now common? Give examples! Is it probable that the vowels had in many such cases ceased to be heard in common conversation? Does Chaucer much use alliteration? Does he seem to have shunned it? Was alliterative poetry still common in his time? Was Piers Ploughman still popular? When was it written? Did Chaucer much use any of the minor artifices of versifiers? (Before, p. 32+, 72+, 85+.) Has this meter been much used by later poets? By whom was it established as "heroic?" (Dryden; *Guest*, *E. R.*, 2, 239.) What did Pope do for it? Is Pope's verse inferior to Chaucer's in variety? Is it superior in any respect? "As far as we have the means of judging, it (Chaucer's scheme of meter) was not only 'auribus istius temporis accommodata,' but fulfilled every requisite that modern criticism has laid down, as either essential to the science, or conducive to the beauty of a versification."—*Guest*, *E. R.*, 2, 238.

Synoptical.—How many nouns have we found with an ending in the nominative singular now dropped? Has any other such ending occurred than *-e*? Is there any peculiarity in the ending of the genitive singular?—of the dative?—accusative?—of the nominative plural?—of the other cases? How many kinds of declension has the adjective? How many examples of the definite declension in the extract? What termination has the plural adjective? Examples? What peculiar forms of the pronouns have we met? What endings of verbs now obsolete to distinguish the modes?—tenses?—persons?—numbers? What peculiar

* * * * * *

With him ther was his sone, a yong SQUYER,
A lovyer, and a lusty bacheler,
With lokkes crulle as they were layde in presse.
Of twenty yeer he was of age I gesse.
Of his stature he was of evene lengthe,
And wondurly delyver, and gret of strengthe.
And he hadde ben somtyme in chivachie,
In Flaundres, in Artoys, and in Picardie,
And born him wel, as in so litel space,
In hope to stonden in his lady grace.
Embrowdid was he, as it were a mede
Al ful of fresshe floures, white and reede.
Syngynge he was, or flowtynge, al the day,
He was as fressh as is the moneth of May.
Schort was his goune, with sleeves long and wyde.
Wel cowde he sitte on hors, and faire ryde.

---

adverbs? Prepositions? Conjunctions? Did Chaucer invent any of these forms? From what language are most of them? Is there any form not from the Anglo-Saxon? Are the Anglo-Saxon and Norman kindred tongues?—with similar forms? Are any endings the same in both? What? (Fiedler und Sachs, 1, 66. Before, p. 103.) Are the endings in Chaucer exactly like the Anglo-Saxon? Do any seem to be a compromise between Norman and Saxon? What? (Marsh, E. L., 384+; E. L. L., 46+.) How many words have changed their accent? Are any of them from the Anglo-Saxon? Why should the Anglo-Saxon accent so suit the English people? (Fiedler und Sachs, 1, 69+.) What words in this extract are not Anglo-Saxon? What is their ratio to the whole number? Is it greater or less than usual in Chaucer? (App. B.) How does it compare with the number in Spenser?—Shakespeare?—Milton?—Bunyan? Were there many reasons why Chaucer should use many words from the French? What reasons for using

He cowde songes wel make and endite,
Justne and eek daunce, and wel purtray and write.
So hote he lovede, that by nightertale
He sleep nomore than doth a nightyngale.
Curteys he was, lowly, and servysable,
And carf byforn his fadur at the table.

* * * * * *

A Clerk ther was of Oxenford also,
That unto logik hadde longe i-go.
Al so lene was his hors as is a rake,
And he was not right fat, I undertake;
But lokede holwe, and thereto soburly.
Ful thredbare was his overest courtepy,
For he hadde nought geten him yit a benefice,
Ne was not worthy to haven an office.
For him was lever have at his beddes heed
Twenty bookes, clothed in blak and reed,

---

much or little Anglo-Saxon can you get from the place in which he lived?—the time in which he wrote?—his rank?—his associates?—his favorite authors?—his education, profession, habits of study?—those for whom he wrote?—his themes?—his character? (Before, p. 35, 87.) Do the necessities of rhyming bring in many French words? What ratio of the whole in this extract are rhymes? Classify the rest of the words not Anglo-Saxon? Are all the kinds of words mentioned in 62? What words in this extract of Anglo-Saxon origin have become obsolete or unfamiliar? What of Norman origin? Of all Chaucer's words, have more become obsolete from the Norman or Anglo-Saxon? (Anglo-Saxon; Marsh, E. L. L., 382.) Did he choose the Anglo-Saxon? (Yes.)—feel with the people?—like their ways and speech? How far is his diction the same as that of Wycliffe? How far is he directly indebted to the language of the Bible? How far indirectly? Is there a diction of poetry in English different from that of piety? What rela-

Of Aristotil, and of his philosophie,
Then robus riche, or fithul, or sawtrie.
But al though he were a philosophre,
Yet hadde he but litul gold in cofre,
But al that he might of his frendes hente,
On bookes and his lernyng he it spente,
And busily gan for the soules pray
Of hem that gaf him wherwith to scolay.
Of studie tooke he most cure and heede.
Not oo word spak he more than was neede;
Al that he spak it was of heye prudence,
And schort and quyk, and ful of gret sentence.
Sownynge in moral manere was his speche,
And gladly wolde he lerne, and gladly teche.

---

tion have the English translations of the Bible sustained to the language of religion? Has Chaucer a similar relation to the poetic diction? Was Chaucer's procedure in the creation of a poetical diction similar to that suggested as Shakespeare's by the questions on page 71+? Which had the wider field to select from? Which had the better preparation for the work? Which has done more for the English language? How does their influence compare with that of the English Bible? (Marsh, E. L. L., 370+; Dwight, i., 136+; Trench, English Past and Present, 36.)

Write an essay on the language of Chaucer covering the ground of the foregoing questions!

APPENDIX A.

ANALYSIS.—Write the sentence in vertical columns. Select the first verb, its subject, object, words connected with it by prepositions, words describing or modifying any of the before-mentioned. Loop the clause by a vinculum at the left, and number the words by figures at the left. Select another verb, its subject, etc.; loop and number: and so through the sentence. Select the leading clause, letter it A, and describe from 404; letter the first dependent clause describing the subject B, and describe it from 409+; and so on through the clauses modifying the subject, verb, and object. Designate on the right of each word the word with which it combines, and the kind of combination. Also, if required, the grammatical etymology, rules of syntax, of orthography, the derivation, kindred words, synonyms, etc.

P. means *Predicative Combination* (405); A. means *Attributive Combination* (406); O. Comp. means *Objective Combination completing* the predicate (407, 408); O. Ex. means *Objective Combination extending* the predicate. The etymological abbreviations in the next column will be easily made out. For the signs in the column of derivations, see page 6. For our example, see page 15.

Clause	Word	Combines with	Combination	Etymology	Derivation
A. Declarative (404).	1. Now	+ 3.	O. Ex.	adv.	<Anglo-Sax. *nu* : Ger. *nun* : Lat. *nunc*.
	2. there	+ 3.	O. Ex.	adv.	<Anglo-Sax. *thar* < *thaet* : : Ger. *dar* <*das*.
	3. were	+ 10.	P.	v. n., ind., imp., 3 pl.	<Anglo-Sax. *vaeron*, ind., imp., 3 pl. of *vesan*.
	4. on	+ 6. } +3.	O. Sign.	prep.	<Anglo-Sax. *on* : Ger. *an* : Gr. ἀνά.
	5. the	+ 6. } +3.	A.	art. def.	<Anglo-Sax. *thaet*> Engl. *that*.
	6. tops	+ 4. } +3.	O. Ex.	n., pl., obj.	<Anglo-Sax. *top*> *tip*, dim. : Fr. *toupie*.
	7. of	+ 9. } +6.	A. Sign.	prep.	<Anglo-Sax. *of* : Ger. *ab* : Lat. *ab* : Gr. ἀπό.
	8. those	+ 9. } +6.	A.	pron.	<Anglo-Sax. See 236.
	9. mountains	+ 7. } +6.	A.	n., pl., obj.	<Fr. *montagne* <Lat. *montana* <Lat. *mons*.
	10. shepherds	+ 3.	P.	n., pl., nom.	<Anglo-Sax. *sceap-hyrde* = *sceap*+*hyrde*.
	11. feeding	+ 10.	A.	p. pr.	<Anglo-Sax. *fêdan* : *food*, *fodder*, etc.
	12. their	+ 13.	A.	pron.	<Anglo-Sax. *thaet*. (See 227.)
	13. flocks	+ 11.	O. Comp.	n., pl., obj.	<Anglo-Sax. *flocc*.
B. Co-ordinate copulative with A (410).	1. and		Connective.	conj.	<Anglo-Sax. *and* : Ger. *und* : Lat. *et*> Fr. *et* : Sansc. *ati*.
	2. they	+ 3.	P.	pron., pl., nom.	<Anglo-Sax. *tha*, pl. of *thaet*.
	3. stood	+ 2.	P.	v. n., str., ind., imp., 3 pl.	<Anglo-Sax. *stôd*, pret. of *standan* : Lat. *sto*> Fr. *été*.
	4. by	+ 7. } +3.	O. Sign.	prep.	<Anglo-Sax. *bi* : Ger. *bei*.
	5. the	+ 7. } +3.	A.	art. def.	<Anglo-Sax. *thaet*> Engl. *that*.
	6. high-way	+ 7. } +3.	A.	adj.	= { high <Anglo-Sax. *heah* : Ger. *hoch*. way <Anglo-Sax. *veg* : Lat. *via*> Fr. *voie*.
	7. side	+ 4. } +3.	O. Ex.	n., sing., obj.	<Anglo-Sax. *side* : Ger. *seite*.
A. Declarative (404).	1. The	+ 2.	A.	art. def.	<Anglo-Sax. *thaet*> Engl. *that*.
	2. Pilgrims	+ 4.	P.	n., pl., nom.	{ Pil-<Lat. *per-*. -gr- <Lat. *ager* : Engl. *acre*. -im <Lat. *-in*. -s <Lat. *-s* : Anglo-Sax. *-s*.
	3. therefore	+ 4.	O. Ex.	adv.	{ there-<Anglo-Sax. *thaere*, dat. of *thaet*>Engl. *that*. fore <Anglo-Sax. *for*> Engl. *for*.
	4. went	+ 2.	P.	v. n., str., ind., imp., 3 pl.	<Anglo-Sax. *vent* <*vendan*> Engl. *wend*.
	5. to	+ 6. } +4.	O. Sign.	prep.	<Anglo-Sax. *to*.
	6. them	+ 5. } +4.	O. Ex.	pron., 3 pl. obj.	<Anglo-Sax. *tham*, dat. of *thaet*.

Clause	Word	Connection	Group	Function
B. Co-ordinate copulative with A (410).	1. and			Con.
	2. leaning	+6.		A.
	3. upon	+5.	+2.	O. Sign.
	4. their	+5.	+2.	A.
	5. staffs	+3.	+2.	O. Ex.
C. Subordinate adverbial with B. 2 (411, III., 5).	1. as	+ 3.		O. Ex.
	2. *to*	+ 3.	$+\overline{4+5}$.	Inf. Sign illogical.
	3. *lean*	+ 2.	$+\overline{4+5}$.	P.
	4. is	+ 5.	$+\overline{2+3}$.	P.
	5. common	+ 4.	$+\overline{2+3}$.	P.
	6. with	+ 8.	$+\overline{4+5}$.	O. Sign.
	7. weary	+ 8.	$+\overline{4+5}$.	A.
	8. pilgrims	+ 6.	$+\overline{4+5}$.	O. Ex.
D. Subordinate adverbial with C. 3 (411, III., 2).	1. when	+ 3.		O. Ex.
	2. they	+ 3.		P.
	3. stand	+ 2.		P.
	4. to	+ 5.	+3.	O. Sign.
	5. talk	+ 4.	+3.	O. Ex.
	6. with	+ 7.	+5.	O. Sign.
	7. any	+ 6.	+5.	O. Ex.
	8. by	+10.	+5.	O. Sign.
	9. the	+10.	+5.	A.
	10. way	+ 8.	+5.	O. Ex.
(B.)	6. they	+7.		P.
	7. asked	+6.		P.
E. Subordinate substantive object of B. 7 (411, 1, 3).	1. whose	+ 3.		A.
	2. Delectable	+ 3.		A.
	3. Mountains	+ 4.	+5.	P.
	4. are	+ 3.	+5.	P.
	5. these	+ $\overline{4+3}$.		P.
F. Co-ordinate copulative with E (410).	1. and			Con.
	2. whose	+ 3.	+5.	P.
	3. be	+ 2.	+5.	P.
	4. the	+ 5.		A.
	5. sheep	+ $\overline{3+2}$.		P.
G. Subordinate adjective with F. 5 (411, II.).	1. that	+ 2.		P.
	2. feed	+ 1.		P.
	3. upon	+ 4.	+2.	O. Sign.
	4. them	+ 3.	+2.	O. Ex.

APPENDIX B.

(From Marsh's Lectures on the English Language.)

In every hundred words, counting repetitions, but not proper names,

Work	Anglo-Saxon words
Robert of Gloucester, Narrative of Conquest, p. 354–364, employs of Anglo-Saxon words	96
Piers Ploughman, Introduction, entire	88
Piers Ploughman, Passus Decimus-quartus, entire	84
Piers Ploughman, Passus Decimus-nonus and vicesimus, entire	88
Piers Ploughman, Creed, entire	94
Chaucer, Prologue to Canterbury Tales, first 420 verses	88
Chancer, Nonnes Preestes Tale, entire	93
Chaucer, Squiers Tale, entire	91
Chaucer, Prose Tale of Melibœus, in about 3000 words	89
Sir Thomas More, coronation of Richard III., etc., seven folio pages	84
Spenser, Faerie Queene, Book II., Canto VII.	86
New Testament:	
John's Gospel, chap. i., iv., xvii.	96
Matthew, chap. vii., xvii., xviii.	93
Luke, chap. v., xii., xxii.	92
Romans, chap. ii., vii., xi., xv.	90
Shakespeare, Henry IV., Part I., Act II.	91
Shakespeare, Othello, Act V.	89
Shakespeare, Tempest, Act I.	88
Milton, L'Allegro	90
Milton, Il Penseroso	83
Milton, Paradise Lost, Book VI.	80
Addison, several numbers of Spectator	82
Pope, First Epistle, and Essay on Man	80
Swift, Political Lying	68
Swift, John Bull, several chapters	85
Swift, Four last years of Queen Anne, to end of Sketch of Lord Cowper	72
Johnson, Preface to Dictionary, entire	72
Junius, Letters XII. and XXIII.	76
Hume, History of England, general Sketch of Commonwealth, forming conclusion of chap. lx.	73
Gibbon, Decline and Fall, vol. i., chap. vii.	70

Webster, Second Speech on Foot's Resolution, entire 75
Webster, Eulogy on Massachusetts in same Speech........................ 84
Webster, Peroration of same Speech 80
Irving, Stout Gentleman... 85
Irving, Westminster Abbey 77
Macaulay, Essay on Lord Bacon 75
Channing, Essay on Milton.. 75
Cobbett, on Indian Corn, chap. xi. 80
Prescott, Philip II., B. I., c. ix.. 77
Bancroft, History, vol. vii., Battle of Bunker Hill 78
Bryant, Death of the Flowers 92
Bryant, Thanatopsis.. 84
Mrs. Browning, Cry of the Children 92
Mrs. Browning, Crowned and Buried 83
Mrs. Browning, Lost Bower 77
Robert Browning, Blougram's Apology 84
Everett, Eulogy on J. Q. Adams, last twenty pages 76
Ticknor, History of Spanish Literature, Period II., chap. i............. 73
Tennyson, The Lotus-Eaters 87
Tennyson, In Memoriam, first twenty poems 89
Ruskin, Modern Painters, vol. ii., Part III., sec. ii., chap. v Of the Superhuman Ideal.. 73
Ruskin, Elements of Drawing, first six exercises 84
Longfellow, Miles Standish, entire 87
Martineau, Endeavors after the Christian Life, III. Discourse 74

If we examine the words in the verbal indexes, and count no repetitions, we find that the total vocabulary of the Ormulum has in every hundred words ninety-seven Anglo-Saxon; the English Bible sixty; Shakespeare nearly the same; Milton, in his poetical works, less than thirty-three. These are the only English books to which Mr. Marsh was able to find complete indexes.

APPENDIX C.

GRIMM'S LAW—*Grimm, D. G.*, i., 584; *Geschichte D. Sprache*, 394+; *Unabr. Gram.*, § 161, 162.

	GOTH. AND ENGL. Smooth.		LAT. AND GREEK. Middle.		GERMAN. Rough.
Labials..............	P	=	B	=	Ph(F).
Linguals............	T	=	D	=	Th(Z).
Palatals.............	K(C)	=	G	=	Ch(H).

	GOTH. AND ENGL. Middle.		LAT. AND GREEK. Rough.		GERMAN. Smooth.
Labials..............	B	=	Ph(F)	=	P.
Linguals............	D	=	Th	=	T.
Palatals.............	G	=	Ch(H)	=	K.

	GOTH. AND ENGL. Rough.		LAT. AND GREEK. Smooth.		GERMAN. Middle.
Labials..............	Ph(F)	=	P	=	B(V).
Linguals............	Th	=	T	=	D.
Palatals.............	Ch(H)	=	K(C)	=	G.

RULE 1.—TO CHANGE ENGLISH TO LATIN OR GREEK.

Change each SMOOTH mute TO its cognate MIDDLE, each MIDDLE TO its cognate ROUGH, and each ROUGH TO its cognate SMOOTH.

RULE 2.—TO CHANGE ENGLISH TO GERMAN.

Change each SMOOTH mute TO its cognate ROUGH, each ROUGH TO its cognate MIDDLE, and each MIDDLE TO its cognate SMOOTH.

APPENDIX D.

The left-hand column has the numbers of the sections in Fowler's Grammar used in the body of this work; the right-hand column the corresponding sections in his large work—The English Language in its Elements and Forms.

1	1	36	61	71	112	106	155	141	197
2	2	37	63	72	113	107	157	142	198
3	3	38	64	73	114	108	158	143	199
4	4	39	66	74	115	109	159	144	200
5	5	40	69	75	116	110	160	145	201
6	6	41	70	76	118	111	163	146	202
7	7	42	71	77	120	112	164	147	203
8	8	43	73	78	121	113	168	148	204
9	9	44	78	79	122	114	169	149	205
10	10	45	79	80	124	115	170	150	206
11	11	46	80	81	125	116	171	151	207
12	12	47	81	82	129	117	172	152	208
13	14	48	82	83	131	118	173	153	209
14	16	49	84	84	132	119	174	154	210
15	17	50	85	85	133	120	175	155	211
16	18	51	87	86	134	121	176	156	212
17	19	52	88	87	135	122	177	157	213
18	20	53	89	88	136	123	178	158	215
19	21	54	90	89	137	124	179	159	216
20	22	55	91	90	138	125	181	160	217
21	23	56	93	91	139	126	182	161	218
22	24	57	94	92	140	127	183	162	219
23	25	58	95	93	141	128	184	163	220
24	27	59	98	94	143	129	185	164	221
25	31	60	99	95	144	130	186	165	222
26	34	61	100	96	145	131	187	166	223
27	35	62	101	97	146	132	188	167	225
28	36	63	102	98	147	133	189	168	228
29	44	64	103	99	148	134	190	169	229
30	46	65	105	100	149	135	191	170	230
31	47	66	107	101	150	136	192	171	236
32	48	67	108	102	151	137	193	172	237
33	55	68	109	103	152	138	194	173	238
34	56	69	110	104	153	139	195	174	239
35	57	70	111	105	154	140	196	175	240

176	241	224	293	272	344	320	397	368	494
177	243	225	296	273	345	321	398	369	495
178	244	226	297	274	346	322	400	370	496
179	245	227	298	275	347	323	401	371	497
180	246	228	299	276	348	324	402	372	498
181	247	229	300	277	349	325	403	373	499
182	249	230	301	278	350	326	404	374	500
183	250	231	302	279	351	327	405	375	501
184	251	232	303	280	352	328	406	376	502
185	252	233	304	281	353	329	409	377	503
186	253	234	306	282	354	330	410	378	504
187	254	235	307	283	355	331	411	379	505
188	255	236	308	284	356	332	412	380	506
189	256	237	309	285	357	333	413	381	507
190	258	238	310	286	358	334	414	382	508
191	259	239	311	287	359	335	415	383	509
192	260	240	312	288	360	336	416	384	510
193	261	241	313	289	361	337	417	385	511
194	262	242	314	290	362	338	418	386	512
195	263	243	315	291	363	339	419	387	513
196	264	244	316	292	365	340	420	388	514
197	265	245	317	293	366	341	421	389	515
198	266	246	318	294	367	342	422	390	517
199	267	247	319	295	368	343	423	391	518
200	268	248	320	296	369	344	424	392	519
201	269	249	321	297	370	345	425	393	520
202	270	250	322	298	371	346	434	394	521
203	271	251	323	299	372	347	435	395	522
204	272	252	324	300	375	348	436	396	523
205	273	253	325	301	377	349	437	397	524
206	274	254	326	302	378	350	437*	398	525
207	275	255	327	303	379	351	476	399	526
208	276	256	328	304	380	352	478	400	527
209	277	257	329	305	381	353	479	401	528
210	278	258	330	306	382	354	480	402	529
211	280	259	331	307	383	355	481	403	530
212	281	260	332	308	385	356	482	404	531
213	282	261	333	309	386	357	483	405	532
214	283	262	334	310	387	358	484	406	533
215	284	263	335	311	388	359	485	407	534
216	285	264	336	312	389	360	486	408	535
217	286	265	337	313	390	361	487	409	536
218	287	266	338	314	391	362	488	410	537
219	288	267	339	315	392	363	489	411	538
220	289	268	340	316	393	364	490	412	540
221	290	269	341	317	394	365	491	413	541
222	291	270	342	318	395	366	492	414	542
223	292	271	343	319	396	367	493	415	543

416	544	446	585	476	615	506	645	536	675
417	545	447	586	477	616	507	646	537	676
418	546	448	587	478	617	508	647	538	677
419	547	449	588	479	618	509	648	539	678
420	548	450	589	480	619	510	649	540	679
421	549	451	590	481	620	511	650	541	680
422	550	452	591	482	621	512	651	542	681
423	551	453	592	483	622	513	652	543	682
424	552	454	593	484	623	514	653	544	683
425	564	455	594	485	624	515	654	545	684
426	565	456	595	486	625	516	655	546	685
427	566	457	596	487	626	517	656	547	686
428	567	458	597	488	627	518	657	548	687
429	568	459	598	489	628	519	658	549	688
430	569	460	599	490	629	520	659	550	689
431	570	461	600	491	630	521	660	551	690
432	571	462	601	492	631	522	661	552	691
433	572	463	602	493	632	523	662	553	692
434	573	464	603	494	633	524	663	554	693
435	574	465	604	495	634	525	664	555	694
436	575	466	605	496	635	526	665	556	695
437	576	467	606	497	636	527	666	557	696
438	577	468	607	498	637	528	667	558	697
439	578	469	608	499	638	529	668	559	698
440	579	470	609	500	639	530	669	560	699
441	580	471	610	501	640	531	670	561	700
442	581	472	611	502	641	532	671	562	701
443	582	473	612	503	642	533	672	563	702
444	583	474	613	504	643	534	673	564	703
445	584	475	614	505	644	535	674		

THE END.

www.ingramcontent.com/pod-product-compliance
Lightning Source LLC
Chambersburg PA
CBHW022143160426
43197CB00009B/1408
9783741186226